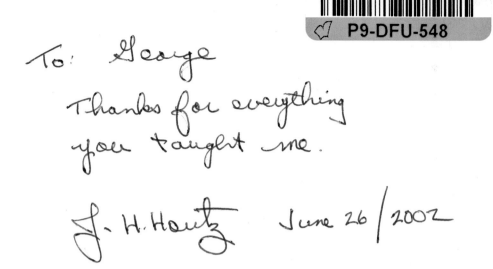

To: George
Thanks for everything
you taught me.

J. H. Houtz   June 26/2002

Seize the American Dream

Seize the American Dream

10 Entrepreneurial Success Strategies

By Jim H. Houtz
with Kathy Heasley

JaGrand

Published by JaGrand Ventures
14988 North 78th Way
Scottsdale, AZ., 85260
(800) 445-9832
(480) 315-0693
www.jagrand.com

Publisher's Cataloguing-in-Publication (Provided by Quality Books, Inc.)
Houtz, Jim H.
    Seize the American dream: ten entrepreneurial success
    strategies/by Jim H. Houtz with Kathy Heasley.
    —1st ed.
    p. cm.
    Includes bibliographical references and index.
    ISBN 0–9717012–0–2

    1. Success in business—United States. 2. Entrepreneurship—United States
    3. New business enterprises—United States. I. Heasley, Kathy. II. Title.

HF5386.H68 2002   658.4'21
                                                   QBI02–200233
Editor and Project Manager: Karla Olson, Via Press, Phoenix, Arizona
Jacket and Interior Design: Liz Trovato, New York City

With Enough Effort

We have all had help
Along the way.
A precise, clear message
Helps define the path.

The old man and the young boy had become friends. How could they avoid it? They lived in the same block, about four houses apart in Sioux City, Iowa. The old man was not too different from many elders who had come before him. He had lived a full life, learned a few things in the process and felt he had more to give. This old man was intent upon influencing the young boy's life, and the young boy obliged him that privilege.

Often the young and the old would sit together and talk. Well, they would tell stories really, with the old man doing most of the telling, and the young boy doing most of the listening. He told the boy stories from his own life; some were exciting and others were not, but nearly all were life shaping.

One day the old man shared a story about his life as an insurance salesman. The young boy braced himself, because insurance didn't sound as exciting as many of the other stories he'd heard. It didn't matter, the old man persisted, and the young boy listened.

"When I was an insurance salesman," the old man began, "I qualified for my company's 100 Percent Club by the end of November with a full month of selling left in the year. They gave me a free trip to Florida." The old man wasn't bragging. He spoke not with pride as much as with determination.

Of course the young boy wanted to hear about Florida, what it was like to see and touch the ocean, to walk on a beach, but the old man went on to explain that the 100 Percent Club awarded salesmen who achieved 100 percent of their sales quotas. And winning it with a full month yet to go was quite a feat!

"So how'd you do it?" the young boy asked.

"It took effort."

The old man told the boy that he was then challenged by his sales manager to do what other salesmen said would be impossible. His sales manager said, "Howard, if you sell another year's quota in December, your wife can go along with you to Florida. It's possible with enough effort."

"Well, that sounds impossible," said the young boy. "It took you 11 months to meet your first quota. How could you sell the same amount of insurance in just one month?"

The old man, Howard, shared his secret of success. "I worked from early in the morning until late at night. I traveled to dozens of homes and made house calls in remote rural areas. I trudged through deep snowdrifts. I scaled barbed wire fences and outsmarted, or just plain outran, fierce dogs. I endured the bitter Sioux City December cold and by the end of the month, I made it. Jimmy," he said, "it just proves that with enough effort, anything is possible."

By now you may have guessed that I'm the Jimmy to whom the old man, Howard, was telling his story of achieving the impossible. The old man was Howard Houtz, my grandfather. I first heard that story at age 12 and at least once a year thereafter until I left for college. Every year the snowdrifts got a little deeper, the barbed wire fences slightly higher, the dogs more ferocious and the December winds colder. Regardless of how big the obstacles got in Howard's story, one thing was always the same: his ending was simply, "Jimmy, it just proves that with enough effort anything is possible."

For Howard, this statement was a foundation for his life. This story and its message were what he had to give. I am thankful that at the age of 12, and for every year thereafter, I had the sense to listen to a story about selling insurance that had the power of a prized fable. I believe that the message of "with enough effort" is one of the principles that successful people follow throughout their lives.

While it is next to impossible to give your maximum effort every day of your life, it is possible to give that extra effort for extended periods of time. And although it may seem grueling, you'll be surprised and proud to know that either you achieved the impossible or that you gave it your best try. Regardless, you'll find you are better for the effort.

I never did learn what Florida was like from my grandfather. But thanks to his story I learned the meaning of "extra effort" and achieved successes that took me to Florida and back many, many times.

Acknowledgments

**Success is not a solo endeavor;
Everyone has had help.
Inspiration comes from many sources,
Fellow employees, family members, and peers.**

The inspiration for this book came from the employees of CyCare and CyData, who were instrumental in helping me seize the American dream of building a corporation from the ground up. They shared the vision, consistently set standards of performance that exceeded my expectations and delivered results for our company and its customers. Through them I discovered many of the insights in this book. In addition, three young, entrepreneurial companies, Excell Staffing, InteGreat Concepts and Southwest Jet Aviation, have proven that the strategies, which were so successful at CyCare, are transferable to other companies, other industries and other business economies. Their efforts and their belief in the strategies for success are very much appreciated.

Special thanks to David Koeller, for his help in defining business issues for some of the chapters, as well as Carolyn Haupert and Phyllis Koeller, who gave their time and talents to provide preliminary edits to one of our early manuscripts. The book would not have been completed without Kathy Heasley, my co-writer, who gave the book clarity, depth and voice, and our final editor Karla Olson, Via Press, whose knowledge and attention to detail took the book to the next level.

It took me six months of nights and weekends to draft the first manuscript. The rewrites took another four months. Without the support of my wife, Joyce, I wouldn't have made it.

Finally, to all the entrepreneurs who have come before me and to all those who will come after me, thank you for your inspiration and for following your dreams. But most of all, thank you for being the living proof that entrepreneurs can do more than start companies. They can run them, too.

Table of Contents

The Entrepreneurial Creed

Do not be afraid of failure;
Be afraid only of not trying.
Look not for fame and fortune;
Seek the inspiration of effort.
Ignore accomplishment applause;
Thrive on achievement.
Focus on an opportunity,
And you are an entrepreneur.

Dare to Dream

We have no greater gift,
Than our freedom to compete.
Turning our vision into reality,
To seize the American dream.

Seize the American dream. It's a simple directive that easily evokes images of financial freedom and success. To many people it is just another way of saying "the good life." But an entrepreneur's definition has a few more facets: specifically, building something from nothing and making a difference in the process. For an entrepreneur seizing that American dream may be quite challenging if a modern-day myth is true. The myth, of course, is that entrepreneurs can only start companies, not run them. You don't have to look too hard to recognize that this tale is founded somewhat in fact. There have been plenty of entrepreneurs who were terrible business people. But there were also plenty who still are among our nation's most admired executives, and their companies are among the most envied. Bill Gates, Steve Case, Steven Jobs, Michael Dell are a few names that come immediately to mind.

So how did they succeed at both entrepreneuring and business management? It's easy to think that the answer lies someplace between super human intelligence, great timing and luck. But their success is really none of those three. The secret to seizing the American dream as an entrepreneur lies mostly with entrepreneurs learning how to manage and grow the businesses they start.

Few if any business leaders are instantly equipped to steer a company to grow from 20 people to 2,000 in the span of a few years. Anyone would be overwhelmed at that task. It requires an entirely new set of skills and abilities. Great entrepreneurial leaders recognize when their companies' success and growth is about to overwhelm them, and in successful companies it gets overwhelming frequently. Know right up front that this anxiety is a sign of growth, not weakness.

Successful entrepreneurs adopt the attitude of the fighter pilot. The fighter pilot is in total control of his plane. He is the one calling the maneuvers. But what separates the great fighter pilot from the true ace? It's not exceptional skill, daring, education or weapons accuracy. Those skills are givens. According to aviation lore, the difference is, amazingly, the pilot's wingman—the guy who flies beside the fighter. A great wingman means a great fighter.

The same is true in business. Smart entrepreneurs make the companies they lead grow as fast as possible and then, as needed, bring on wingmen to handle key aspects of the company. At some point these wingmen (who are just as likely to be wingwomen) become executives who direct such functions as finance, marketing, sales, operations and all the other areas of the company. When the team is in place, acceleration is eminent.

Entrepreneurs spend hours finding better solutions and improving products and services. Oftentimes, entrepreneurs improve people's lives, and in the midst of their continual experimentation, even lower the costs people pay for the things they buy. If it wasn't for entrepreneurs many of the products and services we take for granted today, perhaps even can't live without, would not exist.

Organizations can be entrepreneurial, too. Most of the best ones are. In fact, if history is any indicator, the organizations that maintain their entrepreneurial edge during the next decade and beyond will flourish. Those that don't will be diminished in their wake. The world is in a state of rapid advancement, with entrepreneurs both leading the charge and perpetuating it.

New product and new service opportunities present themselves to all of us on a continual basis, not once in a lifetime. Moment by moment, there are countless opportunities waiting to be discovered and implemented. These opportunities and a healthy dose of inspiration are the foundations of entrepreneurialism.

But entrepreneurial spirit and a viable opportunity are not enough. A true entrepreneur goes one step further. An entrepreneur actually seizes the opportunity by surrounding it with the business practices that will make it a success. This is a challenge a true entrepreneur readily accepts and knows is critical to realizing the dream.

One of the biggest factors of business success is finding ways to inspire people to perform at a high level of productivity. It is the main topic of discussion in management seminars, college courses, lectures, books and articles. Unfortunately, few experts disclose how you actually achieve this goal. The good news is that this book does.

Seize the American Dream tells you how to get started, then it defines the basic business systems that an entrepreneur must have in place to succeed. And it clearly explains how to implement the systems to increase employee productivity.

The entrepreneurial success strategies included in this book did not come out of thin air, nor are they a rehash of the principles you've read about in other business books. Rather, they are the strategies that were developed, refined and hammered out in a real business laboratory called CyCare.

CyCare wasn't really a laboratory, although the company behaved like one. Outsiders saw it as a company that built software administration systems for physician-based group practices and grew to capture a remarkable 33 percent of its market. Insiders, on the other hand, saw CyCare as a company on a continual quest for excellence. The company created, refined, tested and cloned its success and achieved productivity levels beyond imagination.

But this book is not about CyCare. It is about the entrepreneurial strategies that emerged from the lab. Like any researcher, the company made a lot of mistakes before discovering what worked. Improvement was continuous and processes became refined. When something else came along that might be more effective, the experimentation process began anew. There were no linear paths to the company's success. Rather it experienced a number of starts, its share of dead ends, many forks in the road and thankfully a few four-lane open highways. Work continued until the company found the proven strategies that became the hallmarks of CyCare's success. And those strategies are in this book.

Are all the strategies in this book perfect for every entrepreneurial situation? Are they all sure bets? No, they are not. But they are proven, and for each there are four or five alternatives that will not work nearly as well. These are the best practices of the CyCare experiment, and each one of them resulted in higher levels of productivity.

The success strategies in this book are meant to inspire, inform and guide. They are highly adaptable to most business environments and have served as the genesis of numerous successful companies across the nation. This book can be the first step toward finding a source of inspiration and commitment. It may just be the first step to becoming a true entrepreneur and seizing the American dream.

In the Arena

**When will you enter the arena
Where great deeds are done?
Creating value requires a builder.
The courage comes from within.**

With enough effort anything is possible, even the impossible. And to many people becoming an entrepreneur is the impossible. It seems frightening and at the same time enticing, pursuing this American dream. The trade-offs of risk and reward gnaw at every would-be entrepreneur, spurring many to take the plunge and others to recoil into the status quo of their daily jobs. For some, there is that burning desire to get into the arena where great things happen, to be where the real action is, to be on the edge. For others, getting into the arena is about making a difference, doing something important and improving people's lives.

Regardless of the dream, being an entrepreneur is primarily about making something out of nothing. It seems like a larger-than-life task, or at the very least, a ton of work. The thought of throwing caution to the wind, quitting the regular job and going it alone can seem irresponsible, even foolhardy.

It's true that becoming an entrepreneur requires courage. But let's get beyond the ethereal. It also takes capital, a viable product or service and the experience and intuition to implement successful strategies right from the beginning. Contrary to popular thinking, being an entrepreneur means being a builder rather than a creative inventor. The notion that entrepreneurs can only start businesses, not run them is a myth. True entrepreneurs are committed to creating great products and services, but they are also committed to developing and managing the infrastructure that will make their offerings truly successful.

Books can't provide you with the courage to make the leap into entrepreneurialism. You must find that quality within yourself. If you manage to muster the nerve to venture into the unknown, or if you're one of the lucky few who believes right from the start that setting his or her own course is the only course, you'll find this book valuable. That's because this book isn't about helping you decide whether or not you should become an entrepreneur. It's about dispelling the myth that entrepreneurs can't run their own companies. It's about proven strategies entrepreneurs must implement to be successful. Yes, even entrepreneurs follow some rules, although, as you'll find out in later chapters, they break them too.

The first section of this book, called "In the Beginning," covers the start-up phase. It begins by defining the term "entrepreneur." Next it helps you select the right products and services, determine your market and raise capital. The biggest mistake you can make is starting your business before you are ready. Not only does it waste cash and other resources, unless you have a good product or service opportunity and a good start-up plan, you may run out of money before you begin to generate revenue. This section will show you how to avoid the loss of capital and your opportunity to become an entrepreneur and instead seize the American dream.

The second section, "The Success Strategies," outlines low-cost methodologies for each functional area of the company, such as marketing, accounting, sales, human resources and more. It is a no-nonsense look at running a business without the usual complications and clutter. After you have successfully accomplished the start-up phase, you're ready to begin the operational phase and implement the "Ten Entrepreneurial Success Strategies." Two major objectives run through the creation and implementation of these strategies:

1.   **Unique, Simple, Low Cost.** Unique, simple and low cost mean just that. Taking a unique approach to what you do and how you do it will provide differentiation, which is a real competitive advantage. Simplicity will allow employees to do their jobs efficiently and effectively. And low cost operation is critical for all new entrants to an existing industry and for the developers of a new one. Keep in mind that low-cost doesn't mean low selling

price but rather a low cost of doing business. Business is a lot more fun when your costs are 50 percent to 70 percent below the costs of your competitor's. Achieving these simple objectives is an important foundation for success.

2. **Increased Productivity**. The success of any start-up or small company is tied to employee productivity at all levels. Contrary to many first-time entrepreneurs, who believe that buyers make their decisions based on the product or service, the truth is that buyers make their decisions based on a multitude of factors that surround the product. Those factors include marketing, sales, management, customer service, quality, company direction, accounting practices, etc. When everything is working together, the customer's perception is of a company they can trust, a company that will be there, a company that values its customers.

Making all of these areas perform at the highest possible level is the real trick. Certainly it takes an inspired and committed team, but it also takes the effort to inspire and foster a team environment. At some point in your entrepreneurial career, you will decide to make your staff more productive than any other staff you've worked with in the past. When that day comes, you'll unlock the power.

"The Success Strategies" is a "how-to" guide that will help you be unique with simple processes that lower your costs. This guide will also show you ways to increase the productivity and the energy of your team. Now that you've made the decision to get into the arena and pursue your American dream, these strategies will help you excel there.

"Selling Your Dream" is the last section of this book and it covers how to sell your business not once but three times. This is your chance for the big pay-off of financial independence. This chapter will show you how to increase your chances.

From dreams to realities, entrepreneurs experience all the highs and lows of being in the arena. It's a pressure-filled place, but one a true entrepreneur wouldn't want to miss.

In the Beginning

The Entrepreneur

Do your best in all endeavors,
Never quit in the face of adversity.
With enough effort anything is possible,
Success requires intense effort.

Entrepreneurs are special. That's a big statement, but one that is founded when we consider even for a moment just how impactful their efforts have been on our world. From Steven Jobs, who brought us the notion of personal computing, to David Smith and Mortimer Mendelsohn, who initiated the Human Genome Project, each of these special people and the many more yet to come will leave an indelible mark on our society. In business, for example, the efforts of entrepreneurs have filtered through every industry. Everywhere you look an entrepreneur has created some meaningful product, service or process that has made our lives better, lowered the prices of the things we consume and enhanced our workplace productivity.

The first entrepreneurial wave happened at the start of the industrial revolution. Henry Ford set into motion a new way to build a car, the assembly line, which not only produced a better product but also made that product affordable to the masses. He changed the way we build things forever and went on to lead one of America's biggest companies.

Today, we are in the midst of the information revolution. Entrepreneurs like Bill Gates are revolutionizing the way we communicate and share information. As a leader, he built and ran Microsoft, the most successful company of all time. And come tomorrow, entrepreneurs will develop new products, services and processes that our imaginations cannot even begin to conceive today. They'll go on to lead companies that rise to even greater heights than Ford and Microsoft.

But they won't do it alone. In each case, successful entrepreneurs will have wingmen (or wingwomen) by their sides. What are wingmen? They are to fighter pilots the difference between life and death, constantly protecting the leader and communicating threats and opportunities. Every good business leader has a wingman, sometimes more than one. Bill Gates had Steve Ballmer; Ross Perot had Mort Myerson; and Warren Buffett has Charlie Munger. Even small or emerging company leaders have wingmen. Jim Houtz had Dick Burgmeir as his first wingman at CyCare.

Every industry, except those that are eliminated, will find ways to solve their biggest three or four problems and a major portion of the rest in the next ten years. Coming up with the products and services that make these solutions possible will be the easy part. Surrounding those products with a sound business strategy and infrastructure will be the bigger challenge. It will be preserving the entrepreneurial spirit within leaders and their wingmen that will make the difference. Just imagine the possibilities and the potential! For example:

- Imagine a healthcare industry that stores every patient's medical records electronically, allowing automatic updating and retrieval of information anytime. Think of the convenience when access to a physician via email is the norm, and electronic pharmaceutical prescription records are commonplace. Picture worldwide access to the latest medical research, nurses who nurse patients back to health rather than focus on paperwork, and the top ten diseases eradicated.

- Imagine an educational system where every child has his or her own personal computer, where learning at home three days per week and attending school two days per week is the norm. Picture gifted students taking college courses as a regular part of the curriculum in grades one through 12, and schools where every qualified student has access to fast-track courses. Envision schools that are safe from the threat of violence thanks to automatic scanners connected to school security systems.

Imagine, imagine, imagine—that's what entrepreneurs do. But they also do one other important thing: They act. Ideas are a dime a dozen, so the saying goes. It's the actions behind the ideas that require work and effort. Entrepreneurs understand that essential concept, and they go for it anyway. In the years ahead, just like in the years past, the entrepreneurs will be the catalysts of global change. They will see things not as they are but as they could be. They will see opportunities where others see problems. Their inspiration and aspiration will overcome adversity, if not the first time, then for certain on the second, third or the fourth try. The entrepreneur is not deterred by difficulty. A different approach or a more intense effort will certainly bring success. Failure is not an option.

Entrepreneurial enthusiasm and focus inspires people and performance. Pity the underachiever who strolls into an entrepreneur's path. This high-energy environment only has room for commitment and results. Entrepreneurs challenge the best, discard the rest and build organizations that are held in awe by competitors and loved by customers. Why? Because the organizations and the people within them perform.

Don't misunderstand: Entrepreneurs are not perfect. On the downside, they can be so singularly focused that other important subjects can seem meaningless to them. Entrepreneurs think a lot about their businesses, how to make them grow faster, how to build better products and how to improve sales. They also can be espousing the next idea long before those around them have grasped the first one.

Make no doubt, entrepreneurs are different than most other people, but they are an easily definable group that possesses a startling array of similar characteristics. How many of these common entrepreneurial traits do you find in yourself?

- Entrepreneurs do what they do because they are trying to prove or build something; very few are doing it for the money.
- Entrepreneurs usually have above average or super intelligence.
- Behind every successful entrepreneur is a supportive spouse or family and a surprised in-law.
- Fear of failure is the force that drives many entrepreneurs.
- Entrepreneurs don't concern themselves with what others think of them; their satisfaction comes from a job well done, not from a pat on the back.
- They treat employees better than most employers do.
- They are short on planning and fierce on execution.

▶ For them, rules are not etched in stone; they are written to be modified when necessary.

▶ They spend little time on small talk and gossip.

▶ They work harder and longer than any group of people you will ever meet.

▶ Many people consider entrepreneurs risk takers. They are not. In fact, entrepreneurs are simply betting on what they believe to be a sure thing: themselves.

▶ They are singularly threaded and focused on their specific businesses.

▶ Entrepreneurs want to run their companies for the long term. They don't believe the myth that they can't.

▶ Their community activities are usually limited, but entrepreneurs tend to donate generously to worthy causes.

▶ Entrepreneurs can be reasonable in business dealings unless an associate attempts to take advantage of one of their employees. Then an entrepreneur can turn ferocious.

▶ When an entrepreneur goes up against three or four professional managers, the entrepreneur will win every time.

▶ Entrepreneurs are not big on socials, cocktail parties and networking. If someone needs to be contacted, they make the call.

▶ They frustrate other competitors by pricing differently, thinking differently and focusing on execution.

▶ When their dream is sold, they will usually start again. When asked why, the usual answer will be a smirk. They know if you have to ask, you probably will not understand the answer.

There's something endearing about an entrepreneur. No other group will try as hard, risk as much, create as much excitement and do as much good. They are people with ideas who act on those ideas, surround themselves with great people and in the process build a better tomorrow. If you fit this profile, you're in for an exhilarating experience.

2 Opportunity

Opportunity knocks more than once.
It knocks and knocks perpetually.
The sound is like a distant drum roll.
Entrepreneurs select one beat,
And pound it relentlessly.

Everyone knows a few people who always seem to be at the right place at the right time. They take on projects, start new jobs, begin businesses just as a market gets hot. When asked how things are going, they spout out success after success, achievement after achievement. They are the people who leave all the regular folks thinking, "Man, are they lucky. How do I get myself some of that luck?"

Well, for most of these people, save the few who hit the jackpot by winning the lottery, luck has had little or nothing to do with their success. It's not even their knack for being at the right place at the right time. What separates the successful few from the rest of the world is that these people know how to make the most out of any situation that presents itself to them. Are they at the right place at the right time? Of course they are, but so is everyone else. The difference is they are at the right place at the right time, prepared to seize an opportunity.

Clearly, opportunity is as much about circumstance as it is about preparedness. Our ability to recognize opportunities comes from five important sources: education, work experience, industry knowledge, curiosity and intuition. Each of these, to a varying degree, defines our ability to recognize and be prepared to capitalize on opportunities. Let's look at each of these factors in a bit more detail.

Education

Formal education provides the theoretical base that helps us see how tangible objects, intangible ideas and people interact. It provides a big-picture perspective and teaches us how to learn what we need to know to be more aware of the opportunities around us. It also helps us discover those subjects that we find interesting outside of our everyday world, and opens our minds to new kinds of applied thinking.

The best educational background for an entrepreneur includes a college major in a selected course of study, along with a broader educational focus, either as minor or electives, in the following areas of study:

▶ Speech communications

▶ Psychology

▶ Management

▶ Accounting

▶ Marketing

▶ Statistics

▶ Anatomy

▶ Computer science

A formal education that is both specialized and yet broad is a great starting point for entrepreneurial success, but it alone is not enough. Many business experts recommend college graduates work for several years before embarking on advanced degrees. Education alone provides information and theory, but it doesn't necessarily provide perspective. Perspective can only come from work experience.

Work Experience

No matter which rung on the proverbial ladder you begin your career, every job provides valuable work experience in the mind of a true entrepreneur. Every work experience gives the employee a paid opportunity to learn how things really work. At a real job you discover that working is not just about getting the job done, it's about interacting with people; solving problems; fitting in; and, perhaps most importantly learning about your own work habits and skills. These are the internal factors of any entrepreneurial environment.

Young college graduates entering the workplace have an enormous learning curve during their first year of employment. Learning a company's basic procedures takes time and there is no rushing it, despite the demands of our current, fast-paced business environment. New workers need to learn and understand more than the company's product line and key customers. They need to learn and understand the company's language, dress code, business procedures, standards of behavior, performance expectations—in short, the culture of the company. Learning of this type typically doesn't even get mentioned in the classroom environment, let alone taught. These lessons are learned by doing. It is this kind of learning experience—job after job—that provides us with a baseline level of knowledge about the internal work environment with which we can contrast subsequent workplace cultures, processes, products, etc. It is often this subconscious contrast between work environments that sparks ideas for improvement and leads to opportunities. But even if you have a well-rounded education and plenty of work experience, it also takes knowledge of the industry—the external environment—to thrive as an entrepreneur.

Industry Knowledge

Education and work experience paint two-thirds of the picture when it comes to preparing for and recognizing opportunity. Unless you have all three elements, however, you are missing a vital part of the image. Picture a seascape with a sky but no water and no beach. With a beach and water but no sky. It would be difficult for the observer to gain a realistic perspective on what he is seeing. Just as in this simple example, it takes formal education, internal work experience and a solid understanding of the external industry to be prepared for opportunity or even recognize it at all.

Industry knowledge is important to a company's success, so it makes sense that it is critical to recognizing new business opportunities at the entrepreneurial level. Entrepreneurs, just like business people in general, need to understand the external factors that are weighing on an industry. Things like government regulation, consumer activism, labor issues, resource shortages, competition issues are all important factors when gaining big picture perspective. There are numerous other external factors unique to specific industries. When seeking to uncover opportunities there is value in taking a step back and looking at the total image to gain a true perspective. In some cases, it is the only way to see the opportunity before you.

Curiosity

Curiosity, as a human trait, suggests a person who likes to understand why things work the way they do. Many technical people share stories of their childhoods and how they "played" with a new toy. One entrepreneur recounts that when he got a new toy at Christmas, he would take it apart before he ever played with it "just to see how it worked." That was also true for his mother's toaster, blender and any other electrical appliance he could get his hands on. He didn't always figure out how to put it back together, but that's another story.

As much as entrepreneurs love to discover why things work the way they do, an entrepreneurial curiosity goes even further. An entrepreneur's type of curiosity asks, "What if..." And it is the asking of this question, after fully understanding "why," that opens our minds to opportunity. Think about it. Asking, "what if rather than doing it this way, we do it that way?" automatically assumes you have knowledge about the current state of things. The "what if" is the result of our applied knowledge to the situation at hand. These "what if" questions are the beginnings of opportunities.

Unfortunately no entrepreneur has all the answers to these questions. For that reason, the curiosity must extend to a willingness to seek out and find answers to a multitude of questions: How can we apply technology to make mundane processes easier or disappear? What information is available to help us make better decisions? Who says this way is the only way?

It is through increased knowledge and curiosity that we become less accepting of the status quo. We begin to question why things are the way they are more. And we speculate on ways to make them better. Ideas are plentiful at this stage, but it takes intuition to ferret out the most viable "what ifs."

Intuition

An incredible gift we all have, intuition is our ability to know when things are or aren't right. It's the "gut feeling" we have about a situation or person. The most important thing you can learn about your intuition is to listen to it and understand what it is telling you.

But don't confuse intuition with that voice inside your head that tells you why something can't be done. Intuition is not that voice of doubt; rather it is the voice of knowledge that questions an approach, not your abilities as a whole.

Preparedness for opportunity is a function of formal education, work experience, industry knowledge, curiosity and intuition. A real entrepreneur is always learning through each of these conduits. There is no end, because things are always changing. And with change comes opportunity.

So as prepared entrepreneurs, how do you find, evaluate and select an opportunity? Well, there is no one answer to this question, but there are guidelines that will help you in your pursuit. Best of all, they are practical and actionable right now.

There Is No Perfect Opportunity

When you are prepared, as we discussed in the first part of this chapter, you realize that there are countless opportunities presented to us continually. What may not be as obvious, however, is that there is no perfect opportunity. Being an entrepreneur means selecting the best opportunity available at the moment and making it a success. Wavering back and forth between several opportunities or waiting for the perfect one to present itself is a fruitless effort. Select the best opportunity and make it happen.

Knowing the Right Opportunity

There is a great deal of discussion about this topic both from an entrepreneurial perspective and from a career perspective. Current thought is that you should follow your passion and you will be successful. This is partly true, but when it comes to embarking upon an entrepreneurial venture, there are some important elements to consider right up-front—even before passion. They are as follows:

Avoid Big Competition

If your passion is developing computer operating systems, then you might want to see if you are passionate about something else. Who wants to go head-to-head against Microsoft in a battle for its core business? Not a smart entrepreneur. Look at the competition first, then choose a niche opportunity that doesn't compete with the industry gorilla.

Evaluate the Market

Before you get too excited about an opportunity, research the market and the potential market for the product or service you are thinking about offering. The market is defined as the total amount of money currently spent for a product or service. The potential market is the amount of money that would be spent if everyone in your target group bought the product or service you are offering. If the market or potential market is too small for you to operate your company and make a profit, choose another opportunity.

Entrepreneurs often assess vertical markets when exploring opportunities. Vertical markets are a targeted industry segment such as healthcare, banking and insurance. These markets may contain several niches, for example, the healthcare vertical market may contain hospitals, group practices, and teaching institutions. The banking vertical markets may include, consumer lending, commercial lending, and investment banking. There are many more niches in these vertical markets, but you get the idea. Underserved vertical markets can be great opportunities.

Markets have life cycles. There are new markets, emerging markets and mature markets. Emerging markets are surer bets than new markets for a couple of important reasons. First, emerging markets are easier to evaluate for market viability because data on them already exists. Second, emerging markets require less education of the consuming public to gain acceptance. A conceptual sale, which is the sales task in new markets, is always more difficult than a competitive sell, which is the sales task in emerging markets. The competitive sale is a "slam-dunk" if your costs, and therefore your pricing, are lower than those of your competitors.

When evaluating the viability of a market, look beyond just the market's life-cycle stage. Ask yourself about its longevity. How long will this market remain in any one of its phases? How long before it becomes mature and dying? Will I be able to establish a lasting company given this market? Can I build a product or provide a service that has real value over the long haul. As we said in chapter one, true entrepreneurs are not in it for the money; their dreams are much bigger than that. They are not looking for the "Pet Rock" brand of flash in the pan success. They are looking for lasting opportunities that make a difference over the long term.

Be Unique

Why do what everyone else is doing? Do something different, or at the very least, improve on what someone else is doing in a very meaningful way. Avoid the hype of the "next big wave." Often the next big wave never hits, or when it does, it is nothing more than a ripple. Why? Because the real entrepreneurs who weren't buying into the hype were busy developing the products and services that invariably end up usurping the predicted wave.

Consider the multimedia hype of the early 90s. The newspapers told us daily that in the future all our entertainment and our information were going to be on CD-ROM. Video game and content providers were popping up everywhere. Then, out of nowhere came the Internet and its online technology. It all but killed the emerging multimedia industry.

Know Your Passion

A person with a cause is hard to beat. If you have a passion, follow it, but in a way that allows you to fulfill all the other criteria on this list. That means your passion must be tempered with the reality of investors, customers and profit. If fulfilling your passion doesn't seem possible with your current idea—particularly in light of competitive issues, market viability, etc.—get creative and discover a new way to fulfill your passion and still satisfy investors, customers and make a profit.

Talk to Customers

This is scary, actually talking to people you consider potential customers in the early stages of an idea. But if your primary concern is that the people with whom you share your idea will steal it from you, you can rest easier. This seldom, if ever, really happens. The bigger risk involves your ego more than the idea itself. You will need a thick skin. There are generally a lot more people who will tell you why something won't work than will ever tell you that your idea is a winner. In fact, you could come up with a way to mass produce the Holy Grail and people will line up to tell you why it's a bad idea.

Keep in mind that the first person you share your idea with is the hardest, and that it is in your best interest to get over this hurdle. Every entrepreneur needs to discuss the proposed product or service with potential customers, not friends or relatives, in the early stages of development. Here's why. First, prospective customers will often supply real improvements to your idea. They understand the problems your product or service is trying to solve better than anyone. Their honest feed-back is invaluable as you hone your product or service offering.

Second, it is always a benefit to have some customers lined up who are willing to try the product or service upon its release. The goal is to find an early adopter who will take an interest in the project and provide you with a proving ground for your concept. It also helps if these early customers will agree to talk freely about the product or service with other prospective customers.

Finally, talking to potential customers provides clues for product or service enhancements in the future. An entrepreneur, as stated earlier, looks for opportunities that offer long-term benefits. Talking with potential customers is an important way to gain perspective on the long-term direction and opportunities for your company.

Discover Your Motivation

Finally, answer the question "why," and you'll understand your entrepreneurial motivation. Is yours a burning passion to build widgets? Is yours a burning passion to start a company? Whatever your reason, this will give you clues regarding the type of venture that is right for you. Be honest and it will help you weed out opportunities that don't measure up.

Through this insight, the world of opportunities will begin to appear. Take time to evaluate each opportunity using the criteria in this chapter, and you'll soon be ready for the next important step in the entrepreneurial process: Developing the business plan.

The Business 3 Plan

Wait not for the perfect opportunity,
It cannot be found.
Entrepreneurs focus, compete and build,
But first, they begin.

Remember back in college or high school when you were asked to write a term paper? The assignment was to pick a subject, narrow it and then research and write a well-conceived paper that defended and communicated your perspective on the topic. If you were like most students, somewhere between your good intentions and the final paper, you probably looked at what you had written to evaluate whether it was lengthy enough. You may have even held it in both hands and weighed it to decide if the bulk equaled the amount of work you put into it. Perhaps you were checking to see if the bulk made up for the lack of work you put into it!

Consider your business plan the most important term paper you will ever create. Not only is it the document that you hope will garner a great deal of capital to fund the development and growth of a new company, but it is the first document that requires you to realistically examine the business opportunity and commit it to paper. Business plans are not only valuable for securing capital, but also for clarifying your concept and solidifying your thinking. This is the document that helps you figure it all out; this is the time when you determine your plan of action. By the way, the act of putting it down on paper is secondary.

The business plan is where the entrepreneur truly begins to dispel the myth that entrepreneurs can't run their own companies. It's the moment when the entrepreneur makes the decision to build a business, not just a gadget. Hewlett and Packard wanted to build a business before they even knew what products they would sell. They got the garage, started the business and set about figuring out what products to sell.

A business plan is usually a 20 to 50 page overview of the business you either intend to start or the existing business that needs capital, beyond the means of the founders. Too often the creation of a business plan becomes little more than the writing of a term paper about business. Entrepreneurs consider it nothing more than a hurdle to clear or a great way to impress friends and family. Get the business plan written and get on with the work of figuring out the business. That's the wrong approach. Spend the time up-front planning how your business will work, then work it according to your plan. This is your one chance to start on the right course. Thinking your business through now will save you time and money later.

The Reality of Business Plans

The reality of business plans is that few people read them cover to cover. Two sections are most critical: the executive summary and the financial plan. The executive summary is a short, three-to-five page narrative that outlines the entire plan. The financial plan, by contrast, is numbers based and shows financial projections and new capital requirements.

The entire business plan is important, but the executive summary and the financial plan are the two sections most people read. Just the same, write a concise plan making particularly sure that the financials are accurate. Put some extra work and excitement into the executive summary; it's your best chance to get the potential investor to read more of the plan. If you find that very few people read your entire plan, don't feel badly. Chances are they didn't read anyone else's plan either.

Business Plan Outline

What should be included in a business plan? There are many business plan examples on the Internet and in business books, so you should never be short of ideas. There are few sources, though, that reveal outlines for business plans that successfully garnered funding. In general, investors are looking for six important things:

- A good executive summary
- A realistic projection of revenues
- An executable sales and marketing plan

- A viable product or service plan
- A well-qualified management team
- A good exit strategy

The following outline is from an actual business plan that raised $3.4 million and closed on February 27, 2001, during a dramatically down market when venture funds were very difficult to obtain. Take a look at it, and notice several sections that are different from many standard business plan outlines you've seen elsewhere. In your own plan you will likely have industry specific sections. Following an outline specifically is not necessary. Like any other document you create, write your business plan for its audience, making sure it contains all the answers to that audience's questions before they are asked. That's precisely what this plan did.

Business Plan Outline

I.   Mission Statement
II.   Executive Summary
III.   Market Analysis
    A. Industry Overview
    B. Market Drivers
    C. Market Segments
IV.   Business Strategy
    A. Business Objectives
    B. Key Management
    C. Critical Success Factors
V.   Services
VI.   Marketing
    A. Marketing Plan
    B. Image Program
    C. Lead Generation Program
    D. Competitive Advantages
    E. Barriers to Success
VII.   Research and Development
    A. Client Advisory Program
    B. Development Process
    C. Development Meetings and Milestones
    D. Release Cycle
    E. Methodology
    F. Technology
    G. Development Plan
    H. Release Schedule
VIII.   Business Development Strategy
    A. Pricing Strategy
    B. Business Development Forecast
    C. Business Development Plan
IX.   Financials
    A. Financial Plan
    B. New Capital Requirements

Reprinted with permission – InteGreat Concepts, Inc.

This entire business plan consisted of 48 pages and was written by David Koeller, president of InteGreat Concepts. The business plan defined that approximately 40 percent of the funds raised would be used to expand the capabilities of an already installed product, and the rest would be invested in marketing and sales. In short, it showed a minimization of risk and a great opportunity.

When it comes to securing funding, your best chance of success occurs when you are through the product or service development phase and have some installed and paying customers. There's a big emphasis on the word "paying." Unfortunately, having a couple dozen customers using your product or service on a free basis doesn't count. Anyone can give something away, and free usage does nothing to reduce the risk from the investor's perspective.

Business Plan Purpose

If your business plan's primary purpose is to raise capital from professional investors, as opposed to friends and family, you will need a prospectus along with the business plan. The prospectus is a legal document that protects you and the investor. Later in this book you'll learn more about this topic.

The business plan has other purposes than raising capital. In fact, business plans are one of the most important recruitment tools for luring key personnel to your company. Business plans are even useful in attracting those first early adopter customers and will help in obtaining bank financing if you have adequate collateral.

In Practice

Many businesses are started with a business plan that could be written on the back of an envelope, and many of them are very small envelopes. Company founders, however, benefit greatly by spending time thinking through their businesses and all the possible issues related to it. This sounds like a huge task, but it doesn't have to be. In fact, it is better if the entrepreneur doesn't spend too much time on it—perhaps no more than a few weeks. Any business plan that takes more than a few weeks to write is probably too detailed.

After all, the single most important item to an entrepreneur is a customer. Time spent working on a business plan is time spent away from securing customers. There is no greater asset to a new company than a customer who is the first to try the product, pay for it and become a very strong reference. The business plan can help secure that first customer, and that customer, included in a subsequent version of your business plan, will help you secure funding.

Give Investors What They Want

Giving investors what they want doesn't mean giving them large equity positions in your new company. It means giving them a business plan that is viable. There are a few things that investors look for that are worth including in your business plan. First, investors like to see that you have enough capital to get you through the start-up phase. In other words, the business plan you are presenting is designed to raise capital before you really need it. This is attractive to investors. No one likes to deal with desperate entrepreneurs, and desperate entrepreneurs seldom negotiate the best deals for themselves or their companies.

Investors also want to invest in a product or service that is ready to market. Now more than ever, after the crash of numerous Internet companies with great ideas but lacking viable products and viable product marketing strategies, investors want to see a real product or service up-front with a feasible marketing and sales plan behind it. Plans that make sense cannot be understated. Your marketing and sales plan has to be realistic in what it is expected to achieve. Using untested tactics and expecting unrealistic results, for example, will be recognized in a moment and tarnish the credibility of your entire plan. This is your chance to show investors that you know what you are doing. It's not the time to try to mask your shortcomings.

Equally important to the sales and marketing strategy is the total product or service itself. The total product is defined as the product and all the peripheral elements that surround it, such as delivery, service, support, accessories, etc. Investors look for a total product or service in which all the elements of customer satisfaction are well in place. They want to be sure that if your marketing and sales plan succeeds in attracting customers, your infrastructure doesn't drive them away. This certainly was the case with many Internet retailers who successfully attracted customers, then drove them away because they could not deliver the total product experience of on-time delivery and service after the sale.

The business of being an entrepreneur is a people business. Investors want to see a good, solid management team behind any business plan you present. Preferably, your management team should include people who the investors know or who come highly recommended. The implication here is that your best chance at raising money is with an investor who knows and believes in you and your team.

An exit strategy is another important element of the business plan. Investors want to know how and when they will be receiving their investment back plus earnings. Note that an exit strategy in a business plan does not mean retirement at 35 for the company founders. It means liquidity of capital investment. A three- or four-year horizon is most likely, despite the unrealistic trend toward 18-month exit plans. In practice, six or seven years is the norm.

A Word about Vertical Markets

Experts in business have touted vertical market niches as a favorite for new start-ups. Companies that focus on vertical markets select one industry, then develop and market their products or services specifically for that industry.

By focusing on a vertical market you build concentrated market and industry knowledge and rise to expert status inside and outside the niche market. Often you can achieve this status faster than larger competitors who may have found the niche too small to warrant their attention. This strategy also allows you to get a foothold on customers, so that you can own a segment of the market and later migrate your success into other vertical markets. For these reasons, developing two or three vertical market business plans will help you make a more intelligent decision about which ones to enter. Most entrepreneurs learn that business management becomes an issue of alternatives and priorities. Multiple niche alternatives give you a better chance of success.

Keep in mind, you need not hurry to be the first one to market. Windows of opportunity seldom slam shut as quickly as people say they do. Being first is fine, but it is not critical. One definition of a pioneer is "a person with an arrow in his back." It is tempting to forsake business planning for the thrill of business operating. But take the time. Select your industry and products while remembering the Chinese proverb: "A journey of a thousand miles begins with a single step."

Financing the Business

Entrepreneurial risk concerns challenge;
It is not about money.
If success isn't achieved,
Does the courage exist to begin again?

It takes money to make money. This adage has unfortunately kept many would-be entrepreneurs from pursuing their dreams, permanently sidelined, discouraged and unfulfilled. It has also sentenced many existing entrepreneurial businesses to inevitable demise. There are some people who just don't know how to raise capital to fund a business. And then there are those who, thanks to the numerous headlines about start-up failures, class-action lawsuits and venture capital nightmares, are scared to get involved in the whole mess.

In truth, there is some justification for that fear. During the last decade, there was a rash of irresponsible capital investing by both the investors themselves and by the entrepreneurs they entrusted to manage those investments. People in the business of entrepreneuring are experiencing a healthy dose of reality. The result is an investment and entrepreneurial community that is tougher and wiser than ever before.

So how does a budding entrepreneur start building a lasting company if his or her financial condition is living paycheck to paycheck with no cash on hand? How does an entrepreneurial organization venture on to new opportunities if revenue barely covers current operations? Where do you find people who can provide the capital needed to get a business idea off the ground? What are the trade-offs of having someone loan you money? These are all very important questions that nearly all entrepreneurs ask as they wrestle with the question, "Should I, or shouldn't I, follow my entrepreneurial dream?"

The purpose of this chapter is to provide you with some advice about financing your business and offer some financing options worth considering. There are trade-offs with every alternative presented here. That's the nature of the game. We all must give up something to get something in return. When it comes to financing, there are no free rides; everything costs.

Financing Reality

So with that said, there are a few basics about financing that will help you approach it with realistic expectations. The last thing any entrepreneur needs is to become discouraged because the reality of finding money did not live up to the expectation. Here are the facts:

- **Investors Seldom Invest in Ideas.** Most investors are reluctant to invest in a business that represents an idea that you have not yet transformed into reality. One entrepreneur called this phase of a business "the hand-waving stage," because this is the time when you talk to people about your idea and wave your hands wildly to show the grandeur of the opportunity. Investors seldom buy based on hand waving alone. If that's all you've got, continue developing your idea and your company before seeking investors.

- **Investors Like Customers.** Most investors prefer to invest in a product or service that has real customers. Seeking investors before you have a real product or service and real customers is extremely difficult. In those rare instances when you do find an investor, he or she will often demand a very strong equity position in your company. If you don't have any customers for your product or service, you'll want to secure one or more before seeking funding.

- **Investors Like Equity.** Investors will try to gain as much equity in your company as possible in exchange for capital. That sounds like a pretty reasonable request until you look at the long-term implications of giving up 50 to 70 percent of your company in its first run at financing. After all, you have your business to think about, and you'll need the best management team money and stock options can buy. It is imperative that small and start-up businesses reserve adequate equity shares to attract key personnel.

Attracting a solid management team is far more important than money, and handing over too much equity too early to investors can severely jeopardize your chances of assembling the best team. It can actually kill your chances of success.

- **Investors Like Growth.** Investors like entrepreneurs that can grow into business people. They look for qualities of leadership and focus. That's because they know that it takes a leader to turn a great idea into a company with longevity. And it takes a leader to attract the management team, the wingmen that will take the company to new levels of success and achievement.

Bootstrapping

There is no doubt that first-time entrepreneurs tend to think the only way they can get their businesses off the ground is to find someone to provide the cash right up-front. They therefore seek outside capital funding prematurely with unrealistic expectations. Inevitably, it is the rejection and the outlandish requests by investors that devastate the morale of entrepreneurs at this stage in their business development. The important rule here is that entrepreneurs really need to develop the product or service first from their own personal resources, so that when they do attain equity capital, the trade-offs are realistic levels of ownership, not the entire company.

So how does an entrepreneur fund this very early stage of business development? It costs money to get that first customer, doesn't it? There are many large companies today whose founders bootstrapped their businesses to get them off the ground. There is nothing wrong with the rags-to-riches, garage shop recounts of success. In fact, our society romanticizes this kind of Cinderella story. In truth, bootstrapping a company from the ground up is only romantic after it's over. To get a true feeling of what bootstrapping really is, consider this fable:

> *A gentle giant and his wife were walking along in the forest when something terrible happened. In the blink of an eye, both the giant and his wife dropped into a ten-foot hole with no way of climbing out. What was worse, the giant's wife was knocked out cold from the fall. The giant knew he had to do something quick to save his wife and himself before he lost his strength. But what? He looked around, and there was neither a foothold to scale nor a sin-*

gle root to climb. The giant thought for a moment, then carefully placed his unconscious wife across his shoulders. He took a deep breath and summoned a mental picture of effort. He bent over, grabbed his bootstraps and with a mighty tug, lifted himself and his spouse out of the hole.

This story is about a feat that seems impossible. But so are the stories of the many entrepreneurs who started with simple ideas and boot-strapped their way to multibillion dollar companies. If being a successful entrepreneur was easy, everyone would be doing it. Entrepreneurs are required to do what this giant did, and that is to make something out of nothing.

If your true desire is to be an entrepreneur with a significant ownership position in your company, then it is imperative that you find ways to finance the first few steps of the business yourself. You probably have many more resources than you realize.

Once you've pulled your bootstraps for the last time, you'll be happy to know there are other funding sources that will provide the capital you need to get your business off the ground. That's not to say you'll never have to bootstrap again; you will, but there are alternatives. None of them are easy. It takes work, sacrifice and perseverance to harvest the benefits. These sources are described later in this chapter and are listed beginning with "Founder Assets." This should always be your first choice for funding. Each capital source brings along its own level of performance expectations and accountability. Keep in mind the formula:

Performance Expectations + Accountability = Stress

The Prospectus

Before you ask anyone for capital, you'll need a prospectus. As mentioned in Chapter Three, this is one of the most difficult documents you'll ever write. It covers all the reasons and possible ways your business can fail. It is not a marketing document!

Luckily, you don't have to write it. Your SEC attorney has that honor, but he or she will work closely with you. Together, you will draft a document that is designed to put all the cards on the table for you and the investor. It's primary purpose is to protect both parties should things not go as planned.

Finding the right attorney is critical to writing a useful prospectus. Seek out SEC experience. Ask business associates, contact your state

Bar Association and ask for SEC-experienced attorneys. You can even ask your personal attorney.

Founder Assets

The first and most important source of funding is you. Your willingness to invest your cash, sell your house, get a second mortgage is the first test of your commitment to your idea and your company. If you are unwilling to invest your own assets, you may have to ask yourself some difficult questions:

▶ Is my idea something I believe in?

▶ Am I cut out for being an entrepreneur?

When you make the decision to invest your own assets into your business, you'll need to perform a realistic assessment of your worth:

▶ How much cash do I have?

▶ How much is my house worth?

▶ What is my current mortgage amount?

▶ How much cash can I raise with a second mortgage?

▶ What is the value of my other holdings, such as stocks, bonds, and insurance policies?

▶ What other assets can I sell?

Then make an assessment of your business and personal needs:

▶ Can I develop my product or service on weekends and evenings while I maintain my regular job?

▶ Can I handle consulting services while I am developing my product or service?

▶ Can I sacrifice a few luxuries and put the money saved into the business?

▶ Can I work for a lower salary for the first two or three years?

These are choices every entrepreneur must face, but you'll be surprised at how much capital you can raise by bootstrapping. Not only does this kind of self analysis make you more committed to your business, it also shows future investors that you believe in your idea with every fiber of your being. Investors always ask how much you have personally invested. After all, if you do not believe in your project enough to invest, why should they? All partners need to go through the same discovery drill. If they are not willing to invest and sacrifice, why should they be partners?

Customer Financing

Customers are generally not good investors, because they prefer having suppliers who are financially self-sufficient and able to support the product or service sold on a long-term basis. However, once in a while you will stumble upon a customer who isn't afraid to take a risk if the rewards are enticing enough. There are some tried-and-true ways you can approach your customers that will make the customer financing option more feasible.

Built-in Cash Deposits

One method of customer financing is to set up your sales contracts with built-in cash deposits at scheduled intervals. This provides you with a steady flow of capital when needed.

Prepayment for Goods

Another method is prepayment for goods. Particularly with new customers who don't have credit established with your company, this should not seem unusual.

Percentage Completion Payments

When you are providing customers long-term sales or service, set up your contracts so that you collect payments at intervals based on percentage completion, rather than waiting to receive full payment at final completion of the service.

Credit Back Deposits

For service-oriented companies, set up your agreements so that you get more money up-front with the promise of crediting the entire amount against services provided over the next 12 to 24 months.

Using these methods, you can usually receive the full-cost of equipment or supplies that you must purchase to build your product. For service organizations, up-front payments help significantly with salaries and project expenses. Fast growth can demand significant capital infusions. So, with your customers' deposit structures established, you can fund your growth via a continual stream of new customers and make yourself look pretty attractive to future investors—if you even need them.

Leasing

You can improve your capital position by spending the money you do have wisely. Try not to buy anything you can lease. In other words, lease rather than buy computers, phone systems, office furniture, copy machines and more. Cash is king in a start-up—as it is in most other places—and it's difficult to replace when gone. So guard it like royalty. We've all witnessed the gory media coverage showing piles of barely used computers being auctioned for cents on the dollar because a high-flying start-up company ran out of cash and had to shut its doors.

Certainly you want to run an effective company, and you need equipment to do that. If you have three-to-five year leases with realistic purchase options at the end of the lease period, you will have an effective company and you will have retained your valuable cash for those things you can't lease. Even when your company becomes cash-flow positive, leasing is still an outstanding option. Buying anything that doesn't appreciate in value over three to five years is not a good business move.

At some point you will need to lease or purchase office space. It is tempting to buy a building, particularly when lease payments seem extremely high and real estate agents are telling you that if you owned the building you'd be paying toward ownership. Unless you are in the building ownership business, start-up companies need the cash more than they need ownership of a building. You cannot sell your building for fast cash. Before you buy a building or any other expensive asset, make sure you evaluate whether or not that capital could be better used to build a new product or expand your sales program.

Small Business Administration Loans (SBA)

SBA loans are great! You may have heard differently from other sources. Many people feel SBA loans are not worth the time they take to pursue and will try to discourage you from investigating the possibilities. They'll say SBA loans are difficult to get, that you won't qualify for much money or that the paperwork is excessive. Probably the only true claim is that SBA loans do require the completion of a fair amount of paperwork. But this is true for any loan you'll get from a bank or otherwise. Beware of people who will loan you money without paperwork.

You can apply for an SBA loan at most banks, and the leading banks in your community are probably experienced with SBA loans. The application process is similar to that of any other loan, except you complete the SBA information as well as the bank's loan paperwork. The bank then forwards all the information to the Small Business Administration. If the bank approves your application, you'll receive the money and the Small Business Administration will guarantee a portion of the loan. The bank gets a good, solid loan, and you get the cash needed for your business.

The Small Business Administration offers loans specifically for small businesses. If your business has grown to a medium-sized entity, you will be rejected. Bankers who do not offer SBA loans can be very critical of them. Ignore the naysayers, search out competent SBA loan-providing banks, and investigate what's available.

Bank Financing

Banks have two major criteria for lending money:

▶ Proof you really don't need the money

▶ Clear understanding of how you will pay them back

When you walk into a bank and talk to a loan officer, it is easy to get the impression that banks only like to lend to rich people. This is somewhat true. Rich people are safer risks; the likelihood of default is small. But should you manage to secure a conventional bank loan, you'll find another quirk of traditional bank lending. They aren't particularly happy when you pay them back early. The minute you pay them back, they'll want you to borrow again so their loan portfolio does not decrease dramatically.

Banks, like other investors, want to see an existing business in place with real customers. They want to see collateral that guarantees the loan in case of default. Walk into a bank with a portfolio of customers, and they will look upon you more favorably than everyone else asking for cash.

Private Investors

Every community has a group of private investors who will invest in new businesses. Generally, their motives are long-term gain and, in some cases, a desire to be involved with a business they find exciting. Each investor has his or her own criteria, but more often than not the same requirements keep surfacing:

▶ Real, existing products or services in place now

▶ Businesses with paying customers

- A thorough business plan with emphasis on the management team
- A solid exit plan through which they can free up their initial capital investment and a sizeable appreciation on that investment. Exit strategies are usually acquisitions and IPOs (Initial Public Offerings)

There is no easy way to find private investors. It requires networking with other entrepreneurs and community influencers. By talking with lots of people about your business, you will learn who in your community will be receptive to your ideas.

Strategic Investors

Depending on your product or service, you may discover a company that is interested in re-selling your product. They see the profit potential for themselves and therefore have a strategic interest in your success. It is companies such as these that make very good strategic investors.

Strategic investors not only provide capital infusions when needed, but they can also take over a niche in the market that would be difficult for you to tackle on your own. You can subdivide every market into numerous niches; no company can devote attention to every one. Strategic investors, however, can do that work for you and establish your name and product in new markets.

Strategic investors are usually large, established companies. They have the immediate resources to make larger investments in your company and in their own support of your product or service through their distribution channels. Although difficult to find when you are looking for them, often these are the investors who fall into your lap because you have done your business plan homework.

Public Financing

There are a number of public sources for raising capital, but three of them are the most common:

Industrial Revenue Bonds
Industrial Revenue Bonds are funds made available for capital development through state bond initiatives. Each state has its unique definition, and the funds available within each city vary dramatically. You can finance only certain assets with Industrial Revenue Bonds, so that could be limiting to your business. Business people find them attractive because Industrial Revenue Bonds carry lower interest rates than ordinary bank loans. They also tend to be longer term and have favorable

tax treatment. A search on the Internet for Industrial Revenue Bonds in your city and state will generate a great deal of information on what's available. Also, call your local chamber of commerce, in-state investment bank or corporation commission to learn more about this little-known source of funding.

IPOs—Initial Public Offerings

For many entrepreneurs, Initial Public Offerings, or IPOs, are the zeniths of entrepreneurship. Once you achieve this pinnacle, you have "arrived." Many try to arrive too early and find they have killed their promising companies in the process.

Raising money through an IPO requires a very high level of proven success. Specifically, if your business exceeds $20 million in annual revenues, has profitability in excess of 15 percent and a possible annual growth rate of 25 percent or more, you are a candidate for an IPO. If you do not meet all three of these criteria, you'll want to seek other sources of financing.

When your company goes public, everything changes. It often means you are on a rapid growth track, largely the result of stockholder expectations. It means you will implement an employee stock purchase plan. It means financial liquidity for the founders. These changes lead to severe culture and identity transformations. Very few companies are ever the same again.

Going public is a great opportunity as long as you have and can maintain great performance. Wall Street is very unforgiving of companies that do not meet expectations. Not only is it financially devastating, it is like swimming in the ocean with weights attached to your feet. It can be fatal.

Venture Capitalists

Venture capitalists will invest at every level of a company's growth. They can be very helpful or very stressful to an uninformed entrepreneur.

Receiving funding from a venture capitalist requires a business plan and a strong management plan. They will want preferred stock, which on its own isn't stressful, but the conditions included in the preferred stock agreement can be extremely stressful. Beware of the following:

- **Accumulative Dividends.** These are dividends that are payable to the venture capitalist upon sale of the company or an IPO. These dividends can be 10 percent or more on an annual basis. If it takes 10 years to go public, for example, you'd owe the venture capitalist 100 percent of their initial investment in cash. Of course, this is in addition to the preferred stock equity they have in your company.

- **Liquidation Provisions.** Liquidation provisions guarantee that should you sell the company for any reason, venture capitalists (who hold the preferred stock) would receive distributions of the sale of assets greater than the common shareholders (everyone else).

- **Management Matrixes.** Management matrixes are often built into capital funding deals. Should management miss its annual sales targets, the company is required to sell additional preferred stock to the venture capitalists. With a few missed targets, your interest in your own company could go from 50 percent to near zero under this type of arrangement.

Venture capital is a good alternative, but only as a last resort. Try everything else first. Even ask the venture capitalist the unthinkable: Will you take common stock? After the laughing subsides, get back down to business and cut the best deal you can.

Financing your business takes guts. As an entrepreneur this won't be the first or the last gut-wrenching exercise you'll be forced to perform. Know that with the experience-based insights provided in this chapter, your own realistic expectations and a lot of hard work, you will come out on top with enough money to get you and your company to the next level of growth.

The
Success
Strategies

Ten Entrepreneurial Success Strategies

5

Entrepreneuring is about responsibility,
To employees, customers and shareholders.
With the first step, you are committed
To be fully dedicated to your dreams.

An entrepreneurial business is like a 12-year-old adolescent boy. Something is always "out of whack." Some days he feels very grown up, and then in an instant, he's a kid again. Feet and legs are growing faster than the body's ability to operate them. There's awkwardness, but an outward excitement for what lies ahead. Just like guiding an adolescent through those turbulent pre-teen years, guiding a young, entrepreneurial business takes caring, patience, understanding and commitment to keep it on the right track. Perhaps that's why successful entrepreneurs spend on average only 25 percent of their time in their specific areas of expertise, and the other 75 percent of the time taking care of business and keeping everything and everyone moving in the same direction.

Seventy-five percent! Being an entrepreneur is about inventing things, isn't it? Not as much as you'd think. It's more about building a lasting business. In fact, successful entrepreneurs spend a great deal of their time establishing company working environments that foster high employee productivity. They create environments that award productivity, promote innovation, build loyalty and generate *esprit de corps*. They demand involvement and take care of employees with the hope of fostering a winning team attitude.

Entrepreneuring is more than having a vision and a product. It is more than having a business plan and the money to execute the plan—

much, much more. Entrepreneuring is building a company out of people and creating a team out of a group. It's about competing with established firms several times bigger—and winning. It's knowing that people love to compete and to be rewarded for their efforts, not just with money, but with pride for the company and pride for oneself.

The ten entrepreneurial success strategies outlined in the remainder of this book show you how to establish a successful working environment and a winning culture. Of all the elements that come together to build a successful business, none is more critical than the work environment. For instance, having the right product or service is important, but it's not enough. In truth there are thousands of much-needed products or services primed and waiting for an entrepreneur to develop them. Then there's the vision. That, too, is important, but it will change over time. The business plan is needed to define the direction and organization, but it will be constantly modified. Money is a necessity, but money is the least important factor; you can always raise money.

Clearly, the key is the people, those individuals who stand shoulder to shoulder with you and become unbeatable in the marketplace. They are wingmen who treat your dreams and visions as their own and implement the goals of your company as they would their own company. They will perform with confidence, commitment and enthusiasm. To these special people, the entrepreneur owes more than a job. These people have the same hopes and dreams as do entrepreneurs regarding ownership and long-term capital gains. Equity keeps these people motivated and a part of your team.

Peter Drucker, the dean of business writers, tells us the purpose of a business is to market and innovate. The American Management Association encourages CEOs to concentrate on three primary objectives: Plan Ahead, Avoid Catastrophe and Create the Proper Working Environment.

In the last 20 years, Peter Drucker and the American Management Association have been among the most respected teachers of business excellence in the nation. Their advice has helped and guided thousands of business people and entrepreneurs to achieve success. Many entities are indebted to them because their teachings have paved the way to improved performance.

In today's environment, their philosophies are still important, but because of the massive changes in the last three decades, their teachings need to be expanded to help new business entrepreneurs achieve success. What's changed in the last 20 or 30 years? That's simple. Everything! Consider the following:

▶ College students entering the job market have far superior educations compared to graduates of even a decade ago.

▶ Information technology has progressed to the point where every function has become economically feasible and the ROI (return on investment) has become dramatic.

▶ Knowledge levels of all employees have dramatically improved due to the Internet, where anyone can quickly access and distribute information.

▶ The venture capital industry has become huge. Funds are usually available to sound, small businesses, and a good business plan can be funded.

▶ The entrepreneurial wave is of interest to everyone. Ronald Reagan said, "This is the age of the entrepreneur" and facilitated numerous technological innovations during his years as president. Ted Turner said, "This is America. You can do anything here." And as a result, Ted Turner changed the face of media by becoming one of the nation's largest private landholders and dedicating that land to environmental preservation. Everyone knows of someone who changed the world, and now many want to do it themselves.

What else has changed? Look around. The previous five items are only a few of the recent transformations, but they, by themselves, have significantly changed the business environment. In fact, they have changed it so significantly that a business based solely on the teachings of the past will struggle and probably fail.

The Success Stategies

Seize the American Dream promotes ten key philosophical disciplines or strategies that are essential to the success of both start-ups and emerging companies. These are the "how-to's" that turn entrepreneurs into business people. There are no shortcuts. These strategies cover every discipline within your company and have been pounded out through trial and plenty of error in real world companies.

The ten entrepreneurial success strategies are as follows:

1. **A Differentiated Marketing Plan.** Companies stand a greater chance for success if they have a highly focused marketing plan with emphasis on differentiation and lead generation.

2. **An Integrity Driven Sales Process.** Sales must be more than just selling; it must be a process of developing long-term customers by building trust and exceeding expectations.

3. **A Results-Oriented Management System.** Performance is the key, so establishing objectives for every manager and employee sets the foundation for outstanding performance.

4. **A Motivational Human Resources System.** The ability to attract, train and retain highly motivated individuals creates an employee base committed to excellence.

5. **A Resource-Oriented Accounting System.** Accounting must become a resource for company members to create a financially disciplined organization.

6. **A Zero Defects Product Development Program.** The goal is perfection, and the objective is to constantly move closer to the goal.

7. **An Empowered Customer Service Department.** Empowerment of customer service creates a dynamic group who will insist on continual improvements in the product or service.

8. **An Employee-Based Strategic Planning System.** Your employee's creativity will dramatically expand your productivity.

9. **Customer-Oriented Quality Control.** Making quality everyone's priority puts all of your employees on a winning team and builds *esprit de corps*.

10. **Constantly Improving Operations Performance.** The power of information systems and efficient operations can be a powerful competitive advantage.

Entrepreneurs must structure each of these strategies within the company to satisfy the basic textbook objectives for that discipline, but more importantly, to address the motivational needs of the entire employee staff. Our primary challenge as entrepreneurs is to create a cadre of personnel who are highly motivated and operate with a high degree of enthusiasm and efficiency in a transformed business environment.

One of the most famous football coaches of all time, Knute Rockne, was said to be able to convince his players that they could run faster than they really could, that they were bigger than they really were and that they could play better than they really could. He did it by teaching the fundamentals, assigning responsibility and developing a high degree of pride and *esprit de corps.*

Your entrepreneurial challenge is to develop this same level of pride and spirit while creating a productive, positive and highly efficient employee base. If your ten, 15, 100 or 500 employees are average performers, you'll have an average company and, in due time, disappear. If your employee team is highly productive and you can be two to four times more efficient than your competitors, then you have a chance. Working hard is important, working smarter is better, but working harder and smarter is best.

The ten entrepreneurial success strategies will provide a foundation for developing a highly productive team. But before launching into the strategies themselves, realize that when you enter the entrepreneurial world, several truths become evident:

- There are no more free lunches.
- Decisions are made right or wrong by the manner in which they are executed.
- Your most important asset is a customer, and it's your job to take care of that customer.
- Your efforts will determine success or failure.
- It's not the critic who enters the arena.
- Life isn't always fair.
- The harder you work, the luckier you get.
- The only thrill greater than being an entrepreneur is being a successful entrepreneur.

Some think being an entrepreneur is about finding a killer product and pursuing it. That's certainly part of it. The professional entrepreneur knows the real test is convincing others to accept the vision or the combined vision and together creating the work environment that makes the dream a reality.

As you grow in your entrepreneurial career, when your ideas become products, which become sales, which become user assets or tools, when you review your accomplishments and say "I did that," then you are on the path to success. When all of your employees can say, "We did that," then you have arrived and are successful. You will have achieved an inner sense of pride and accomplishment greater than anything you will ever imagine.

A Differentiated Marketing Plan

Vision is the essence of marketing.
Great deeds are fueled by imagination.
Choose the less-traveled path,
And find ways to touch all mankind.

Enroll in even the most elementary of marketing courses and within minutes of buying your books and receiving your course syllabus, you'll discover one of the primary principles of marketing—the Four Ps: product, price, place, promotion. They are the foundation of all marketing decisions and the key variables that differentiate one company from another. You, the entrepreneur, may have all four Ps in your marketing plan, maybe even more than four, and certainly more than your competitors. But that's not enough. Quantity does not imply quality. When it comes to marketing success, as well as overall business success, the quality of your marketing plan and the Ps it contains is defined with one word: differentiation.

To successfully market any product or service, no amount of money or salesmanship will replace, in the long run, a solid marketing plan in which you have included the appropriate variables and implemented them properly. And "properly" means that these variables must differentiate you from your competitors. Of course, it is easy to understand the importance of differentiation if you enter an existing market. You must differentiate yourself to get noticed, plain and simple. The same is true if you are innovative enough to enter a new market and savvy enough to develop a leadership position. Your success will draw others. As competition heats up (and it will), your task of differentiating yourself will begin, like it or not.

Many entrepreneurs are surprised to learn that developing the product or service is the easy part of the job. The real work comes after you have a product or service that differentiates you from the others in the market. The next mission that you must tackle is determining how to obtain customers and revenue for the business.

Unfortunately, it is true that developing the product is the easy part—and in many cases, the fun part—of the entrepreneurial process. The real work comes from selling your product and servicing your customers. It can be baffling and overwhelming if you ponder the scope of these tasks for too long. For some it can be overpowering enough to extinguish their entrepreneurial fires altogether. But that doesn't have to happen, especially if you take the next step and develop a differentiated marketing plan for your blossoming business.

Most entrepreneurs, who are not necessarily marketers at heart, go first to the marketing textbooks referenced in the beginning of this chapter. They seek out the textbook approach hoping that by being technically correct they will be right—and if you recall, right means differentiated. Sadly, most marketing plans in those textbooks are based on companies with far greater resources—money, personnel and time—than the typical entrepreneur who is in the start-up mode. Perhaps the venture capital funded dot-coms of the late 90s were able to implement, in many cases unsuccessfully, the textbook marketing plan model. Today, the real world entrepreneur, with a start-up marketing budget of $5,000 to $200,000, has to be more realistic.

If the dot-coms have taught us anything, the lesson learned is that more money doesn't equal more success. All the Super Bowl commercials in the world will not buy loyal, happy customers who are there for the long term. It requires far more thought, far more planning and far more work to be successful. It takes a differentiated marketing program that covers the following areas:

- Market selection
- Purpose of marketing
- Product or service differentiation
- Pricing differentiation and positioning
- Promotional differentiation
- Distribution channel selection
- Personnel

Let's review each of these sections in more detail.

Market Selection

The first decision point in any marketing plan is the selection of the market. Who will use your product or service? Is it a consumer-based sale or a business-based application? So, the first exercise in developing a differentiated marketing plan is defining your market. This includes defining the type and numbers of buyers, as well as their geographical proximity to your primary location.

One of the most common mistakes made by small and start-up businesses is trying to please and serve everyone. The temptation is great, especially in the early stages of business development. As long as money is coming in the door, it is natural to assume that all business is good business. Still, the tendency to compete in too many markets can cause a company, already limited on resources, to lose focus and fail. Instead, entrepreneurs should select one market and focus all of the organization's efforts, including sales and business development resources, on that one market. Dabbling in other markets may seem like a great strategy that will improve a company's chances for success, but in fact the opposite is true. The drain on the organization can often be fatal.

Some products and services are suited to multiple markets. How does any entrepreneur choose and choose correctly? If you do have several markets that are viable candidates for your product or service and you are having a difficult time selecting one to focus on, ask yourself the following questions:

- How many prospects are in each market?
- What are the growth rates of the businesses in the market?
- What is the geographical proximity of these businesses to my business headquarters?
- What is the percent penetration of my type of product within each market?
- Who are the main competitors in this market?

The answers to these questions will guide your decision of which market to choose first. It's a big issue and one worthy of much thought and investigation. Using the questions above as your guide, you'll be able to uncover the facts that will lead you and your growing company in the right direction. Of course, regardless of the market you choose, your product or service must offer worthwhile benefits to its buyers. It must be differentiated from competitors or other products that solve similar problems. Without these important attributes, the market you choose will not matter.

Contrary to popular belief, it is actually easier to market a viable product or service within an existing market than it is to market the same product in a new market that has no competitors and no existing users. When you look at today's industry leaders—Intel, Cisco or Microsoft for example—you realize the first mover hypothesis is a myth. Very few of today's most successful industry giants got there by being the first to enter an industry.

When selecting your market, pay special attention to the last item on the checklist: the market competitors. This is an extremely important consideration when selecting a market. Are you ready as a company to compete head on with General Electric or America Online? Can your resources win out in a head-to-head fight? If you can't answer yes to these questions, competing with these industry gorillas may mean your company and your product or service will have a short life span. What you may be able to answer affirmatively is that you can compete with the big players in very select niche markets. As long as you offer something that benefits your buyers and positively differentiates your product or service, you have a chance. But get ready to dodge some bullets!

Purpose of Marketing

There is often much debate about the purpose of marketing. Increase sales, build brand image, satisfy consumer needs and many other purposes are routinely discussed at length in books, at seminars and in conference rooms around the world. Regardless of the validity of any of these marketing purposes or the dozens of others not mentioned, marketing has one ultimate purpose in an entrepreneurial organization. That purpose is very different than the marketing purpose in large or even mid-size companies because an entrepreneurial company must focus on only those elements that will deliver the biggest pay-off.

In an entrepreneurial company, marketing's primary purpose is lead generation. Granted, you will need to develop product brochures, web sites, sales tools, contracts, training materials and a host of other support materials, but lead generation is the single most important function of marketing in an entrepreneurial organization. You should assign the bulk of your resources toward achieving this objective. If funds permit, outside contractors and professionals can handle developing the other materials. Or, if money is limited, your weekends and evenings are available at no charge. Apart from who handles the other tasks, the primary responsibility of marketing is lead generation, and it is an important variable in determining your marketing pay-off.

How does an entrepreneurial company quantify "pay-off"? First, plan to evaluate your marketing in terms of return on investment related to the market you intend to attack. Your resources will always be limited and usually tied to a fixed dollar amount, or even better, a percent of revenues. Obviously a percent of revenues becomes challenging from a planning perspective in very young companies that have no customers or a limited number of customers. Planners then must rely on reasonable projections and forecasting to guide their marketing investment. Pay-off is the return on investment calculation that equates leads generated with dollars spent to generate those leads. The lower the cost per lead, the better the marketing.

In fact, lead generation is so important that if your marketing activities during the normal business day of 7 a.m. to 6 p.m. aren't generating leads, stop doing those activities.

Product or Service Differentiation

Did you ever stop to look at the phone on your desk? Most likely you have buttons for everything: transfer, hold, conference, park, music, call following, forwarding and many more. Phones today are highly feature-rich. And phone manufacturers go out of their way to add more frivolous features in a desperate attempt to differentiate their products from those of their competitors. (What is "park" anyway?) Do phone manufacturers understand this is an effort in futility?

Entrepreneurs need to realize that, although it is fun to design and develop features, features do not differentiate products. The primary differentiation for any product or service lies within the benefits to the user of that product or service. Competitors easily add on features to products, but the competitive advantage lies in the delivery and communication of the benefits. In 90 seconds or less, you should be able to recite with passion the three most important customer benefits. And the way you say it must be easy to remember and unique.

When developing this 90-second or less "elevator speech," as it is often called, you can ask yourself how your product or service helps customers...

‣ Solve their problems?

‣ Control their growth?

‣ Take advantage of new opportunities?

‣ Make their lives better, easier, happier?

Through questions such as these, you will begin to understand how your product or service benefits your customers. You'll be able to separate the benefits from the features and differentiate your products in the most meaningful way.

Pricing Differentiation and Positioning

Contrary to the trend in the late Nineties, when many dot-com companies believed that profitability was optional, profitability is crucial to business growth and success. Profitability means companies can continue to invest in product development, research and market expansion, which is a win for both the company and its customers.

The single most important factor in profitability is price. Because of this relationship, price is a critical element for a company's long-term viability. Unfortunately, pricing is often misunderstood. In fact, many companies are structured to fail because of inappropriate pricing. Look at start-up technology companies; they often price themselves into a gloomy future. Typically, these entities sell their products for significant up-front costs and charge 5 to 15 percent of the purchase price annually for maintenance on those products.

This pricing model is highly dangerous at best. Companies that embrace this pricing structure are expecting the front-end selling prices to supplement maintenance revenues, which are too low in the first place. They are banking on continual sales increases to finance the operation and growth of the company. If at any time sales drop off or stall because of the economy, competition, personnel loss or any other problem, revenues could easily drop below the current cost level. That is not a favorable position. Consider the alternative: Establish the purchase price lower and price maintenance at 40 percent to 60 percent. Think of it as a modified leasing program with significant up-front revenue.

With this model you have the potential to receive notably more revenues over five years, three to four times more revenue in six to ten years and generate a revenue stream, which will enable your company to grow and prosper. With well-conceived pricing, everybody wins. Your company grows and becomes more successful, and your customers invest in a product that continues to be supported and improved.

As part of your pricing structure, you need to factor in appropriate discounts and stick to them. However, flexibility can pay off. You may find a prestigious prospect that would make a highly valuable customer from a public relations perspective. Prospects with strong images are clients you need to win. The power of their brand name will rub off, and you'll gain more business purely by association. Don't give your product or service away, but be prepared to discount in exchange for linking your company to this prospect's high-profile image and reputation.

With customers, big or small, strive for long-term, five-year contracts where appropriate. Long-term contracts are always better than short-term (one year) contracts or no contract at all, because contracts represent revenue you can count on for your company's operations and growth. As a word of caution, when developing contracts, be sure to include cost of living increases and some type of volume increases.

Now that we are clear on the importance of appropriate pricing strategy, how do you go about determining the actual selling price of your product or service? Most pricing methodologies are driven by cost, competition, the needs of the industry in which you operate, your business's income stream structure and your business philosophy. Pricing is also determined by emotional factors such as how badly you want to win the business you are seeking.

Price must have a relationship to the cost of producing and marketing your product or service. Your accounting staff can identify the price you'll need to charge to achieve the necessary gross margins. But this "accounting-determined" price is not the "differentiated" price you'll want to promote to be successful. You need to determine a simple unit of pricing that is meaningful to the market to which you are selling. Some simple units include number of users, number of concurrent users, number of trucks, per system, per package, etc. Whatever meaningful differentiated pricing you choose, you'll want to keep in mind your profitability goals. Your differentiated price should always meet or exceed the accounting-determined price.

Promotional Differentiation

As in the other areas of marketing, differentiation in promotions is critical to success, and two major factors affect promotional differentiation. They are your promotional message and the media for that message.

Promotional messages must differentiate and communicate benefits and results to the reader. Messages must contain real reasons that will motivate a reader to take action, and show the uniqueness of the offering as compared to the rest of the market. Too many messages stress the advertiser's image and neglect motivating the reader to take action. Over time, your promotional message will change. Resist all attempts to soften the message by eliminating the differentiation aspects. Keep in mind that verbiage about technical features is just that, verbiage, and it belongs in a technical manual. Differentiate your message by making it unique, and stress the benefits and the results.

Media selection can be baffling, particularly if you have not adequately targeted your market and the audiences within it. The confusion fades fast when you realize that media selection is directly related to the size of your market and the dollar amount of the typical sale. If your market is a small market and your product or service has a high unit price, direct mail is an excellent first choice. If your market is large and your unit price is small, a consumer marketing approach with public relations and mass media advertising is a solid media strategy. Obviously, there are many shades of gray in between these two extremes, but both show the relationship between market size and price. You can and should support all promotional efforts with user testimonials and other media where appropriate.

Small niche markets, the kind in which entrepreneurs typically enter, pose great opportunity for one-to-one marketing. This type of marketing is highly relationship-based and requires budgets for tactics such as personal letters and direct mail. In many cases, letter campaigns have garnered higher response levels than glossy direct mail campaigns, because letters are less often screened as junk mail. A large percentage of direct mail brochures never make it past the mailroom. Personal letters are seldom screened.

Distribution Channel Selection

When developing your business plan and initial financial plans, consider how you will actually get your product or service in the hands of your customers. In other words, what distribution channel will you use to get your product out in the market? There are several types of distribution channels and each has advantages and disadvantages as well as different profit-and-loss attributes. Here are the most common channels from which you can choose:

Company-Employed Representatives

The term "company-employed representatives" is another way of saying company sales force. Many companies have their own sales forces and enjoy a number of benefits from this distribution method. First, company-employed representatives are captive, focusing solely on your product or service. You have a great amount of control over what they say, what they sell and what they ultimately deliver to the customer. You also are not competing for the attention of sales representatives who are selling a host of other companies' products.

On the down side, company-employed representatives are expensive. An inside sales department can cost a company a significant percentage of every dollar they sell. That's the trade-off for the luxury of control and undivided attention. Company-employed representatives can be split into two categories, with the first one requiring the largest ongoing investment:

- **Direct Sales.** This is your typical, on-the-road sales person who meets face to face with prospects and clients. This method works well when you are asking customers to make a large investment or purchase or when more consultation is required to make the sale. There's no substitute for personal interaction.

- **Tele-sales.** Also called telemarketing, this method involves trained sales representative on the phones following up on leads and making cold calls to sell your products. This is often used for low-cost or commodity products and services or when the sales message is simple enough to be explained over the phone.

Some organizations employ both of these models using tele-sales to qualify leads, for example, and direct sales to meet with the qualified prospects face to face. Others use direct sales to sell the primary product or service and tele-sales to sell any supplies or add-on services. There are a number of configurations for this distribution channel. The key is matching the right one to your product and your customers' needs.

Indirect Channels

In some instances, companies do not want an entire in-house sales force that sells directly to the customer. They would rather sell to a larger number of people at a discount, and let them in turn sell to end customers in higher volume. The benefits are greater revenue potential and rapid sales deployment. The primary drawbacks are lower profit margins and a lack of control. In essence you are selling wholesale and are no longer the direct link with your ultimate customer. In some instances the trade-offs are worth it. There are two primary types of indirect sales:

- **Value Added Resellers (VARs).** Use this channel when your product or service is included as part of another vendor's offering. The VAR can then take your product or service, package it as part of a total solution (thereby adding value) and sell it to the customer.

- **Dealers/Agents.** Dealers or agents represent many products or services within a specific industry and within a small geographic area. The key to success with this channel, which is more suited for smaller transactions, is keeping the dealer/agent's attention and providing ongoing training.

The Internet

The Internet has been touted as the great equalizer because companies of any size can have a sales presence online. While online sales continue to grow, they are growing at a slower pace than predicted in years past. Nonetheless, the Internet is a primary distribution channel for many companies and an alternate channel for almost all others. It has appeal because it can take you directly to your customers without the need for an intermediary sales force—direct or indirect.

As Internet technology stands now, it can play a major role in distribution, with some important limitations. The Internet is a good channel to sell products or services that are commodity in nature. It also is well suited for products and services that involve frequent repeat purchasing and where customers can serve themselves. A well-designed web site that makes it easy to buy, and a company that provides exceptional follow-up are absolute necessities for success in this channel, which will continue to mature in the coming years.

Each of these three types of channels requires extensive sales training. Your own representatives and the indirect representatives all need sound foundations to be successful. In addition, the indirect channels will require sales personnel to recruit all the various types of resellers. And yes, even the Internet channel will require ever-increasing numbers of people building industry alliances and providing real-time, online sales assistance.

Personnel

You can run a very efficient support organization for sales (either direct or tele-sales) with a limited staff. Initially, you may not need a director of marketing if either you or your vice president of sales possesses the marketing experience to get this function off the ground. Another option is to enlist the services of a reputable advertising agency or marketing professional who can do the work on a contract basis.

In most young companies, two telemarketers and one database manager should be able to generate leads for six to eight sales people. Telemarketers are in place to respond to inquiries from lead-generating mailings and to make outbound market research calls. Telemarketers also send the information to prospects who want to learn more about your company and its products or services. This group would be trained to spot a viable prospect and turn it over to the sales department for follow-up.

When it comes to marketing, there is no substitute for differentiation. It must become the basis for your messaging and be integrated into everything you do. You will get tired of hearing this same product or service differentiation message long before your customers and prospects will. Actually, some experts say that when you are growing weary of saying the same thing over and over, your target audience is just beginning to catch on! Stick with your commitment to differentiation and become its champion.

An Integrity Driven
Sales Process

Sales people are your warriors.
Attract the best and give them training.
Teach integrity to build long-term relationships,
And positive results will be the reward.

Every job is easier when you have the right tools and the knowledge of
the process. It's even easier when you have experience so you know
what to expect and how to respond. Ask any weekend do-it-yourselfer.
Repairing that broken garage door, installing that much-needed irriga-
tion system or building bunk beds for your kid's room can be relaxation
or massive frustration depending upon your tools, your knowledge and
your experience.

This chapter is about outfitting yourself for selling your product or
service to your various markets. By introducing yourself to the
Integrity Driven Sales Process you'll gain the knowledge, the tools and,
over time, the experience your sales team needs to be productive.

A quick glance at a thesaurus shows that the word "integrity" is synonymous with honesty, truthfulness, reliability and honor. Integrity
Driven Sales is an honorable way to assist others in making the best
purchase decision about a product or service.

Integrity Driven Sales is not about fast talk, faulty claims, slick deal
making or pushy closes. Those were the sales techniques of yesterday
when making the sale was all that mattered. Never mind the destruc-
tion to your company's reputation, brand name or product image.
Unethical sales tactics worked fine when customers had fewer choices
and fewer places to turn for the same or similar products and services.

In today's world no company is so omnipotent that it can treat customers poorly and not have its reputation tarnished and its future business hindered. On the contrary, there is always somewhere else people can go to get almost anything.

Not only will an Integrity Driven Sales Process grow and retain a positive reputation for your company, it will also make you unique in any industry and differentiate you from the competition. Integrity Driven Sales is an oxymoron to some, and you're probably thinking if nice guys finish last, why would I want to be nice? To the entrepreneur who is striving to build a strong company for the long term, Integrity Driven Sales is a foundation to the all-important differentiation we discussed in the last chapter. And in case you're still concerned about finishing last, rest assured. Studies show and experts agree that a business' survival over the long term is dependent on developing long-term relationships with customers. Not the superficial relationships of decades past when a good sales rep knew the names and birthdays of all their customers' kids. We're talking about value-added relationships that help the customers and their companies grow and prosper.

Value-added, integrity relationships are built on the trust that comes from establishing realistic expectations on both sides of the desk. The ultimate goal of this kind of relationship is a partnership where both partners win and where the resulting solutions created produce real benefits. This is the opposite of blue sky selling where the answer to everything is, "We can do that," without regard to that small detail called the truth. Disappointment and serious backpedaling are inevitable. Integrity Driven Sales, instead, discloses accurately the product or service's capabilities and outlines realistic return-on-investment opportunities. There is no need for blue sky. There is no need for wild exaggeration. You have a viable product and a realistic business plan, right? So who needs to lie?

Truth in sales is unique, but when you are the honest person for whom everyone is searching, the world will beat a path to your door. If you develop an Integrity Driven Sales Process, you will have differentiated not just your sales but your company as well.

Guiding Principles

In case you're wondering how people who practice Integrity Driven Sales think and behave, here are some of the principles that guide them on a daily basis:

- Take care of the customer and everything else falls into place.
- Fulfill your commitments to customers, other employees and yourself.
- To be successful, do what you say you will do.
- The customer is always right.
- Set appropriate customer expectations.
- SWAT: Sell what's available today.
- Be true to yourself.
- Be true to others.

It probably sounds like the suggestion is simply to be a better person. That is true. Taking the high ground places you above the rest. Every company wants a sales team that is fiercely driven to win and to succeed, but when it comes to selling, the end doesn't justify the means. Great companies win by adhering to the rules of Integrity Driven Sales, and in the process raise the level of consumer expectations that all competitors must live up to. That makes it pretty tough for the competition, particularly if in addition to your integrity, your company also offers superior products and delivers more value.

In small companies the founder and the president must set the example. In larger organizations it may be the vice president of sales and marketing. Regardless of the title on the organization chart, Integrity Driven Sales starts at the top and becomes part of the company culture. It is a conscious decision that rapidly becomes a performance expectation for all employees.

The Intellectual Challenge of Selling

Sales is a profession best suited to competitive, self-motivated, smart people who are good communicators. At least that's what everyone says. Many people think you're either a born sales person or you're not. With Integrity Driven Sales, that is not really true. There are plenty of successful Integrity Driven Sales professionals who don't fit the classic sales representative profile of a shark who goes after the almighty dollar. In fact, many of the best sales people use their intelligence rather than simply their drive to be extraordinarily successful.

The challenge to all Integrity Driven Sales professionals is to use their intelligence with every sales situation. Every sales situation is different, and approaching each one with intellect gives your sales team the ability to recognize the real prospects for your product or service and what it will take to make a prospect a satisfied customer. Customer satisfaction begins with the sales process, not once the product is sold and in the customer's hands.

The intellectual side of Integrity Driven Sales qualifies the prospects, determines their possible objections and crafts a solution to solve customers' needs and fulfill their objectives. Nowhere in this scenario are the tactics of overwhelming the prospect with facts or twisting their arms. The intellectual aspects of Integrity Driven Sales is the foundation for adopting this philosophy and requires all sales professionals to use their brains instead of their brawn, their wisdom instead of their wits to get the order.

So how do you find these special people who can take the high road and use their intelligence to understand their prospects? It's not easy, but here are a few tips on sales team recruitment.

Sales Team Recruitment

As a typical entrepreneur you are probably too busy to screen applicants for sales positions, but you absolutely must interview the finalists. In fact, thinking of your sales team as sales representatives is very misleading. You are recruiting company representatives. They are likely to be the first human contact people on the outside will have with your company, and they represent you, your products or services and everyone in the company. To the prospect, they are your company, and like it or not, prospects and customers will form opinions about your entire organization based on the actions and intentions of your sales representatives. In any interview, ask yourself, "Would I take pride in this individual?" Answer it honestly based on behaviors, attitudes, appearance and values. If you cannot answer yes, move on to another candidate. You only get one chance to make a first impression, and 80 percent of the time your sales representatives make it for you.

Finding the right people is difficult. It's a mistake to recruit sales people only when you need them. Recruit everyday and everywhere, every minute, through friends, associates, colleges, competitors, at seminars, in airports or wherever you happen to be. If you run across someone who seems to have the integrity and the intellect, ask a few questions and set up a meeting. Not an interview, exactly, but a get-acquainted session that is designed to determine "fit." If a person fits in, you can teach them the rest. By searching thoroughly, hiring selectively and training extensively, half of the sales people you hire will make it. You'll need to quickly, but gracefully, assist the other half in their exit so they can pursue other career opportunities in which they can be successful. That's part of the integrity as well—helping others be the best they can be in your organization or elsewhere.

Sales Toolbox

Just like our weekend Mr. Fix-it at the beginning of this chapter, the job of selling goes more smoothly with the right tools. For the sales representative, those tools are knowledge and information rather than a hammer and saw. Every successful sales person must be armed with a collection of company documents that together constitute a complete toolbox.

These documents are designed to assist the sales cycle and frequently reduce the sales-cycle time. They are essential in creating an effective sales team and to delivering a consistent image of your company and its products or services. Here are a few examples of what the typical toolbox contains:

Product Brochures

These simple documents describe your products or services and their related benefits. Sometimes called fact sheets or data sheets, these are separate documents for each product or service. The rule with product brochures is to keep them simple and benefit oriented. Too often companies try to put too much information in these sheets. Remember, as the number of words increases, the number of readers decreases.

Technical Write-Ups

These documents are more technical in nature and include specific information about the capabilities, features, companion products (yours or other companies') and expected results of your product or service. These are critical to technical selling where decisions are made based on integration into existing infrastructures. The more complex the product or service is and the more difficult its implementation, the more you'll need technical write-ups.

User Write-Ups or Case Studies

User write-ups or case studies are very powerful sales tools because they function two ways. First, they act as a user testimonial that proves what you are offering actually works and is in operation somewhere.

Second, they let prospects identify with the real life stories of people just like them. The typical format for this type of document is to describe the customer's problem. Define how the customer had been addressing it, if at all. Discuss the shortcomings of those methods or the challenges of doing nothing. Then describe how the customer used your product or service to solve the problem. Within this outline, you must substantiate your company's claims regarding benefits about the product or service. It's also much more powerful if you can show in general terms some kind of bottom-line results for the customer.

Company Brochures

Company brochures frequently become mammoth projects. One marketing consultant revealed that out of ten projects that never make it to the press in one year, seven of them are company brochures. It's common for companies to become frustrated with their generalness and want to make them more complete with more detailed product descriptions, etc. Then the brochure gets too large, costs escalate, company details change and the project never gets done.

The reality is, detail is not the purpose of a company brochure. Rather, it is a simple document that is designed to foster credibility and familiarize prospects with the company. Instead of trying to say it all in your company brochure, include the company's mission, a letter from the CEO or founder talking about the company's customer service and quality philosophies, pictures of company facilities and a broad overview of all company products. If you are a young company, keep mentions of customer names to a minimum so you are not handing over your client list to your competitors.

Price Book

Develop an easy-to-update, simple price structure for your products or services with emphasis on recurring revenues, volume breaks and appropriate discounts. Pricing needs to be clearly documented for two important reasons. First, you want to make sure you are treating every-one fairly. Second, comparative documentation comes in handy when showing value-added incentives such as free accessories, free services, or discounts from the list price.

Return-On-Investment (ROI) Guide

Most products and services sold to business entities have a return on investment. Strangely enough, most sales people sell features and underestimate the power of a good ROI analysis. Help your sales team by giving them an outline of the quantifiable economic benefits of your product or service, and show them how to calculate the value for every selling situation.

Proposal

You can create a standard proposal for most products or services. There are a number of sections that can stay the same regardless of the prospect, and others that you'll need to customize based on each situation. The standard sections include:

- Company overview
- Company capabilities
- Product/service description
- Personnel capabilities
- Installation/implementation steps

These sections require customization:

- Cover letter
- Executive summary
- ROI analysis
- Price/offer section

Customers should not be left to review proposals without a sales representative present or present on the phone. That is suicide. Most entrepreneurs would be dumbfounded if they knew how many of their mailed or delivered proposals are never read. It's probably over 80 percent.

Contract

Professional companies have a structured contract. Look at model contracts, make a list of what you'd like to have in your own company's document and work with an attorney to draft one. In general, it should define deliverables, payment terms, maintenance costs, cost of living increases, limits of liability, contract terms and renewal provisions. Plus anything else your lawyer says you need. Your contract should be fair but also complete. A thorough document will help you avoid significant catastrophes. It is easy to feel that a handshake is good enough, but keep in mind that there is no protection in a handshake, and should problems arise, it's your word against your customer's. Guess who's always right?

Sales Training

Americans love football and its heroes. Ask any football fan to name the most successful college coach and Bear Bryant will surface immediately. People talk fondly of the Bear, because he had what it takes to get the most out of his 11 players on the field. In fact, they used to say Bear could take his 11 and beat your 11. And then take your 11 and beat his 11. How was that possible? It was possible by focusing on the fundamentals of football.

If you thoroughly train your team on the fundamentals of sales, you can beat anyone: IBM, Microsoft, GE, your two biggest competitors … anyone. Why? Because knowledge is the cornerstone of Integrity Driven Sales and, surprisingly, few companies are focusing on fundamentals! It seems clear; you need knowledge to be truly responsive to customers' needs. When you respond to customers' needs, you build trust. Through trust, long-term relationships develop, which leads to a stronger business and more sales.

Keep in mind sales training is necessary for whatever distribution channel you select. Company representatives, indirect representatives and your Internet representatives will all require extensive training.

Some may feel that indirect and Internet channels will eliminate the need for sales training. In reality, they reduce sales costs but increase the need for sales training. Company representatives who know your company inside and out and have a long-term understanding of your products and services can overcome many company deficiencies. Without their presence, however, you are reliant on training programs for proper representation.

To ensure that your sales integrity—and your company integrity for that matter—are maintained, plan on spending more for marketing materials and sales training with indirect and Internet channels than you would spend with a direct channel. Indirect sales channels need collateral to assist in the communications process and build your credibility with the reseller or agent as well as the actual customer. The Internet requires all materials to be available online. To maximize this channel, it is important to have sales assistance available 'round the clock via a toll-free phone number. After all, your doors are always open online.

Through a solid focus on teaching and learning sales fundamentals, you may not win every sale every time, but you'll win your fair share.

A sales training program based on fundamentals should include modules on the industry, products/services, sales cycle, and sales techniques, at an absolute minimum. Let's review these in more detail:

Industry Training

Almost every industry has unique terminology and characteristics. To be effective in any industry, your sales people need to use the correct terminology and have a clear understanding of how the industry is structured. Especially important is knowledge of the basic problems facing that industry and knowledge about solving those industry problems.

For companies with products that cross industry lines or that serve multiple industries, you'll need training for each industry. Some companies develop small note cards for their sales people that identify the industry's terminology and its key business methodologies, issues and solutions. Today, those notes can be loaded into electronic handheld organizers.

Many of the best sales people in any industry are those individuals who take the time to learn how to communicate in the prospect's language and the language of the industry. The only way to communicate with integrity is to learn everything there is to know about the industry itself. The language will come with the knowledge.

Product Training

Some sales representatives ask, "How much do I need to know about the product?" The answer is simple: everything! It is the company that must facilitate that learning. A comprehensive product/service training program is a cornerstone in sales training and will spill over into the areas of customer service, new product/service development throughout your company.

A comprehensive review of the product or service is essential to Integrity Driven Sales. It's the only way your sales force can develop into trusted advisors to their customers. Comprehensive means understanding the origins of the product or service, knowing all the features through hands-on sessions, learning how the product or service interfaces with other products or services, and understanding any shortcomings. That's just the beginning!

Sales Cycle

A sales cycle is the time it takes for a prospect to turn into a user of your product or service. It includes the initial interest—perhaps a cold call—and ends with the use of the product or service and the payment for it. Every product or service has a sales cycle. Your company's sales cycle may be very short, very long or some-thing in between based on the complexity of your product or service, its price and the nature of the companies you call prospects. The length or brevity of the sales cycle has nothing to do with the success or failure of a company. On the other hand, not knowing or under-standing the sales cycle can be devastating. Only by knowing your sales cycle and sharing it with your sales team can you develop realistic training and set realistic expectations for yourself, your sales representatives and your company.

Similar products have similar sales cycles. Two manufacturers of jet aircraft will have the same sales cycle. A maker of computer networking equipment will have a similar sales cycle to that of a producer of enterprise software. If your business is new, you can gain clues regarding your company's sales cycle by looking at similar or competing products, asking future customers what would be involved in making a decision to purchase, etc. As you develop your training module for the sales cycle, use the information you gained from your research, and focus on these sales-cycle steps:

- **Initial Interest.** A prospect's initial interest is usually the result of a direct mail inquiry, media advertising, public relations coverage or telemarketing cold call. The sales department receives the lead and makes the determination who will follow-up. Sometimes the lead is a request for more information. If the sales department has the information, they may send it, but the best approach at this stage is to make a quick qualifying phone call, particularly if the lead is with a company or in an industry you are targeting specifically.

- **Demonstration.** On-site demonstration will frequently be necessary at a later time, but today our technology has enabled us to openly demonstrate our products or services without being present. By using the Internet, companies can demonstrate their products (services to a lesser degree) effectively and efficiently with no travel cost and no time lost. While sales literature may direct prospects to view the online demo, this second phase of the sales cycle is frequently prospect-initiated fact finding. The prospects themselves are determining whether or not the product or service is compelling enough to pursue further. It is a highly effective way to gauge a prospect's level of interest. If the prospect viewed the demo and is calling your company or is receptive to a sales rep's call, he or she is probably more interested than someone who has not taken this much initiative. However, for as wonderful as the technology is, most products and services will still need a face-to-face demonstration, particularly when multiple decision makers and users exist,but this would come later in the sales cycle.

- **Qualification.** The biggest difference between inexperienced and experienced sales people has to do with qualification. Qualification is the process of determining the viability of a sales prospect. The young sales person thinks everyone is a prospect, tries to work every single lead and achieves marginal success. The experienced sales person, on the other hand, determines, through asking qualifying questions, who will be the first movers in the territory and then focuses on the best three or four prospects.

  Qualification, like so much of the Integrity Driven Sales Process, happens by asking questions in an open, non-threatening manner. These questions may include:

  ▶ Do you currently use any products similar to our product?
  ▶ Are you currently looking at products similar to our product?
  ▶ When do you intend to begin evaluating these kinds of products?

Plus other key questions posed by senior people in your company.

We all talk about prioritization in business. Qualifying leads is no different; it is really a process of prioritizing. Yet it is amazing how many companies do not qualify sales leads. Poor qualification or lack of qualification results in wasted efforts, wasted money and wasted time—all energy that your sales team could spend securing real business. Sales forces that don't qualify leads will seem extremely busy and will often say they have "a lot of business in the pipeline." Through training, help the sales team understand the difference between leads and qualified leads. A pipeline full of qualified leads can launch your company to exponential growth. A pipeline full of unqualified leads can leave you spinning your wheels in a quagmire.

- **Needs Analysis.** Also called a system study, needs analysis is usually required to help prospects see the value of the product or service you are offering and to help you learn everything you can so you can make better recommendations. Needs analysis projects are investments of time. You would not want to perform this type of study on an unqualified prospect. The goal of the needs analysis is to determine how your product or service fits into the organization, not if it fits in. You should already know it fits before the analysis, through the qualification process.

  At this stage, your sales force needs to understand how to be both consultants and sales representatives at the same time. This is a delicate balance that takes integrity and finesse. If you are fortunate enough to be selling in one vertical market with a product or service targeted to that market, your sales team probably has done a similar system study before. In this instance, the systems study becomes more of a selling process, with the sales representative speaking from a position of wisdom and knowledge. Your training for this stage must emphasize the need for each sales representative to develop internal champions for the product or service within the prospect organization. These champions will help the sales rep get the information you need to make an effective and viable recommendation.

  When you have a technical product or service with high dollar sales potential, the 80/20 rule applies. You'll find that the 20 percent of the sales representatives who understand the power of a needs analysis will sell 80 percent of the business. Is it because they are natural born sales people? No. It's because they took the time to get to know the prospect and his or her needs. It's because they are building value-added business relationships.

- **Proposal and ROI.** The next step in the sales cycle is the sales proposal and the ROI or return on investment. By now, the sales representative should know enough about the company and its needs to develop a proposal that hits the mark and an ROI that is meaningful and realistic.

This may sound familiar from the business plan section of this book, but the two most important parts of the proposal are the Executive Summary and the ROI. You may recall the two most important parts of the business plan are the Executive Summary and the Financials. We live in a world where people want the facts and people want to know how much it costs! Realize that and your sales team will be ahead of most. Make these two sections brief, yet compelling and, above all, valid. If your prospects like the summary and the ROI, they will delve further into the proposal.

An ROI that is full of holes only shows how much you don't know about your prospect and can destroy your chances of success. Every sales representative needs a champion within the prospect company to help craft and validate the ROI analysis. From the systems study, the sales rep has collected the necessary information to develop a compelling ROI. Keep in mind that most CEOs or buyers will assign projects on a priority basis. Those items that have the greatest ROI (in percent and absolute terms) will command his or her greatest interest. This is not a license to blue sky your ROI. It is a license to instruct your sales force to do their homework and discover every possible point of savings and return.

- **Site Visits or Reference Checks.** In many sales situations, particularly technical ones, a visit to the prospect's location is an important and valuable investment. It may happen before or after the proposal stage, and it may take the form of several visits. Your sales force needs to understand the objectives of site visits. First, a site visit is an opportunity for sales representatives to meet face-to-face with the prospect. This is the chance to take the business relationship to higher ground. A relationship can only go so far over the phone or through email volleys. The face-to-face meeting is an opportunity for the relationship to flourish.

Another important objective of the site visit is to show your product or service in action. This is the prospect's opportunity to see the product, touch it, plug it in, push the buttons. For service-related site visits, this is the chance for the prospect to see how the sales representative works and acts and helps the prospect decide if there is a "fit" between the two companies.

The site visit is reference selling at its best. In many cases, the prospect is comparing your company, its products and services, to others that he or she is reviewing. Consciously or subconsciously, the prospect is setting up reference points from which to compare your product or service offerings with others. How you measure up defines if you win the business or lose it.

- **Contract Review.** How often in sales is the contract the deal breaker? Things are moving along so well, relationships are developing, there's great anticipation in both organizations, and it all comes to a crashing halt because of the contract. Sometimes the damage is so devastating that the company never recovers from it and loses the business. Other times, the contract gets tied up in legal departments almost permanently.

  There's a simple way to keep this from happening. Train your sales force to review the contract agreement with the prospect before the close. In fact, make a point to include it in the proposal. If time permits review it during the proposal presentation. Do it as a manner of information disclosure as opposed to an attempt to close the sale. This will give everyone time to talk it over, understand the content and negotiate any areas of concern.

- **Closing the Contract.** Many sales training programs teach students to ask continually for the order during the sales process. For most products in today's business environment, this is inappropriate. It is certainly inappropriate in the Integrity Driven Sales model. This philosophy of "trial closing" is based on coercion, trickery and relentless persistence. A sales representative may succeed in beating a person down and getting the sale, but in most cases, he or she will have jeopardized a lasting business relationship.

  It is appropriate, however, to ask for the contract at the right time. The right time is after the prospect reviews and affirms the ROI and after the sales representative has answered all of his or her objections. At this point, asking for the order can be as simple as saying, "We have presented all the material and all of the facts, it's time for you to make a decision. We would like to have you go ahead with the program." Notice that the close technique is straightforward and honest. It is not the game playing that is characteristic of other sales methods and counter productive to Integrity Driven Sales.

Based on this statement, the prospect will say in some way or another, "yes," "no" or "not yet." Be prepared to ask, "Why not?" in a polite, non-accusatory way. These are critical junctures, and if your sales representatives handle the rejection with grace and understanding, they will greatly improve their chances of turning a "no" or "not yet" into a "yes."

- **Installation.** The sales cycle isn't over with a signed contract. In fact, it isn't finished until your company installs the product or delivers the service promised and the client is satisfied. Companies often falter at this stage in the cycle with the transition from the sales representative to the product or service implementation team. Too often sales representatives perform disappearing acts and move on to the next hot prospect. When this happens, the customer can feel "dumped," which jeopardizes the long-term relationship. Your sales training must stress the importance of keeping the sales team involved until customers are fully comfortable with the implementation team. Show them how to do this with grace. Often this means taking a back seat and facilitating trust building between the implementation team and the client. It can be a bit like the job of an ambassador. A company that cannot effectively release its sales force to sell will severely limit its growth opportunities. This is a critical skill to master.

Understanding and working within your industry's own sales cycle is not a matter of choice. It is based on your customers timeline, not your own. Experience is the best teacher, and, over time, your industry's sales cycle will become your own. It will guide nearly everything you do.

The Sales Funnel

The sales funnel is a graphic representation of the ideal path a sales process takes from start to finish, beginning with "sales suspects" and continuing through prospects to customers. The funnel also serves as a foundation for frequent philosophical discussions, heard in many company sales offices, about the role of the sales person. Everyone knows the sales representative's primary responsibility is to close sales. That is undisputed. The question arises when one asks, "What should the sales representative be doing the rest of the time?" Should he or she be...

1. Converting more suspects into prospects by taking them through the qualification process or

2. Concentrating time and effort on the prospects already in the funnel?

Most individuals automatically say that sales representatives should concentrate on the prospects in the funnel—choice number two above.

Miller Heiman, a well-known and well-respected sales training company, says the opposite. They believe that sales representatives should spend their time moving suspects through the qualification process into the prospect funnel. This is particularly true for technical sales applications. If your company is targeting a particular industry or market, eventually handling prospects within the funnel becomes routine work. Proposals are quite similar, ROI analyses are similar, contracts are similar. That's just one of the benefits of market focus. It is, in fact, the suspects who need the attention and qualification to fill the funnel. If your sales force can keep your funnel full of qualified prospects, they will work more efficiently, and your company will hit revenue targets. If your sales force fails to keep the pipeline full, closing the sale will take as much time as is available—often a great deal of time—since there are no other prospects to run through the sales process. An empty funnel breeds inefficiency. Keep your funnel filled with prospects, and your sales force will be productive, motivated, encouraged and probably quite rich!

Sales Techniques

There have been volumes written about sales techniques, many with diametrically opposing views. There is very little to say about selling techniques that has not been said thousands of times, but there are techniques that are fundamental to Integrity Driven Sales. Each of these techniques is related to a simple directive of this selling method.

Ask Questions and Listen

Most sales representatives talk too much. Not just a little, but a lot. Worst of all, they talk themselves right out of the running. Perhaps the tendency to talk too much is a result of excitement and ambition. It

Sales Funnel

may be nervousness. It could be a personality trait. Regardless of the cause, you must stop this problem in its tracks.

As we discussed earlier, Integrity Driven Sales isn't about fast pitches or show and tell. It's about honestly and openly discovering ways to help a prospect. We were all born with two ears and one mouth, so we should be listening twice as much as we are talking. Particularly early in the sales process, when sales representatives need to get prospects talking about their problems and their objectives. Let customers tell their stories and when it is time to respond, do so with integrity.

Answer Objections

Objections to your company's product or service benefits will arise. Collect them, develop answers to them, and publish them so your sales force knows how to respond. During the sales process, ask clarifying questions so that there is a solid understanding of the prospect's objection and why he or she made it. Frequently you can turn objections into reasons for purchasing just by clarifying the problem and responding. Objections are real, so don't let your sales representatives ignore them. They must address the objections head on and with honesty to alleviate the prospect's concerns. It's actually a good idea to ask right up front, "Did that address your concern?" If it did, move on. If not, ask more clarifying questions. This is an exercise in discovery more than selling.

Avoid Arguments

Some prospects, perhaps by their nature more than the situation, can be very argumentative. In cases such as these, practice good customer service skills. Stay calm and let the prospect talk. Getting rattled or trying to fight back is a no-win proposition. Clearly, the way to win respect and build relationships with people who are argumentative is to rise above the situation with calmness and professionalism.

Avoid Losing Your Temper

Some people and situations can bring out the worst in anyone. Your sales representatives will encounter some tough people and some tough situations. Integrity Driven Sales and selling in general dictates that there is no appropriate time to lose your temper. In short, if you lose your temper you automatically lose. Period. No second chance, no recovery, you are out. No one is going to deal with someone who has temper tantrums.

Create Visual Pictures

It's always a good idea to use visual pictures when describing your product or the environment in which it is used. The more you can help the prospect picture the benefits happening in their own world, the better. You understand the prospect and the needs. The prospect deserves to understand your vision for how things could be.

Make It Easy to Buy

Have you ever encountered a company that doesn't want your money? Have you ever felt that you were practically throwing the dollars in their laps and they were tossing them back? It's amazing, but some companies actually make it hard to buy by designing stumbling points into their sales process. For example, asking prospects to review and sign multiple contracts instead of rolling everything into one itemized agreement is an invitation for delays. Look at your sales process through a prospect's eyes and experience all the hassle points. Eliminate them, make the purchasing process easy and your sales will increase.

Make It Hard Not to Buy

You're probably thinking we covered that in the last item, but making it easy to buy and making it hard not to buy are two different things.

Making it hard not to buy is about communicating a compelling argument and putting forth an offer the prospect can't refuse. This isn't to be confused with deal making, but rather the process of doing your homework and arriving at an irrefutable solution with a great ROI that the prospect would be a fool to pass up.

Handle Multiple Decision Makers

In Miller Heiman's business classic, *Strategic Selling*, they explain that in many sales situations, you will encounter multiple buyers. Those buyers usually include:

- CEO or management
- CFO or accountant
- CIO or consultant
- User group

When this is the case, you'll need to understand the objectives and address the objections of each person.

Manage Multiple Unit (Branch) Sales

Frequently, selling your product or service is a two-step process:

1. Sell the home office, and
2. Sell each branch or plant location

Know the dynamics of the prospect company. In 90 percent of the cases, you'll need to sell the home office on the product or service before you can sell the branch offices. Once the home office is on board, the door is open for you to aggressively pursue all their entities. Sometimes sales representatives will say they can sell the branch first, then the home office. This is unlikely particularly for enterprise products or services. Experience dictates you work the home office first or work them together.

Setting up your sales organization is a time-consuming, work intensive, iterative process. It will challenge your entire range of skills and experiences. A good sales team and good sales people are a result of selective recruiting, great training, a comprehensive sales toolbox, an emphasis on ROI and handling growth, and a compelling desire to succeed. The Integrity Driven Sales Process model helps make all these things possible.

Know that despite your best efforts to do everything right, you will make mistakes. You'll make bad hiring decisions, and you'll forfeit golden opportunities. More opportunities will come your way, but it's the people who count the most. When you find good sales people, give them plenty of support, tons of encouragement, plenty of freedom and stand back. Don't lose them; they are rare and very valuable. In reality, one or two superstars can make a small company great. They also can teach and inspire others. They in essence become the standard by which you judge every other sales representative in the company. By using Integrity Driven Sales you'll be setting a very high standard, a standard that is worthy of your new company and its future customers.

A Results-Oriented Management System

Management is the foundation.
Leadership provides the light.
Performance is the key,
Which drives us to success.

The key to Results-Oriented Management is maintaining a company-wide focus on performance. Performance must come from each individual—each supervisor or manager, each officer and each functional group. Building an effective management team is far easier than you may expect if you build it based on a management system that is oriented toward performance. Results-Oriented Management stresses performance based upon leadership, management by objectives, training and integrity, all of which are reviewed in this chapter.

There isn't a manager alive who hasn't at one time or another daydreamed for just a moment about how much easier work would be if people weren't involved. Just imagine...doing the work you love...making a difference...succeeding...all without the office politics, the incessant interruptions, the questioning of decisions, in short, all the things that make work, well...work. If you think too long, the bubble bursts rather abruptly, because you quickly remember you are only one person and you can't do it all. You need a wingman and staff. Businesses need people—temperamental, emotional and unpredictable as we are—to survive and, in truth, to thrive!

Enjoy the isolationist daydream while it lasts, but when you return to reality understand that the dream workplace isn't one without people, but one with people who are managed by results. Entrepreneurial management is different than traditional management. In addition to all the other things at which you must excel, you as the entrepreneurial manager must lead, train and inspire. Let's not forget you are working with very limited resources and a clock that is ticking loudly in your ears. Before you know it, larger competitors will be breathing down your neck. There's no time for a dress rehearsal. You and your team have to "get it right" the first time.

Does that mean that every decision you make has to be perfect? Not at all; that's a lot to ask of anyone. In reality, you will make important decisions but not always perfect ones. For that reason, it is crucial that you instill in the people around you an intensity of effort and the highest of expectations to be successful. Think about your current work environment. A perfect plan, implemented poorly, results in what seems like a bad decision. Average decisions, by contrast, implemented enthusiastically and with intensity can generate brilliant results. The difference is one of effort and expectations.

In large companies, managers have the luxury of implementing several solutions and selecting the best alternative. An entrepreneurial company with limited resources and limited time does not have this kind of luxury. Your company leaders will have to make decisions and run with them. Running with them is called "intense execution."

How do you get employees to give 150 percent when in most work environments it seems like companies are lucky to get what's left over from a rough weekend on the town? The commitment to intense execution effort comes from a group of managers and employees who are working for a cause rather than a paycheck. It is a group that has committed itself to the company vision and a pursuit of excellence.

Read about any successful entrepreneurial company, and you'll find recounts of execution-oriented people throughout. You'll even find stories of them in unsuccessful entrepreneurial companies, which in all likelihood failed for reasons other than its people. Look for and develop people who are motivated toward a cause. Of course that means you have to hire selectively, but more importantly it means you must teach people what they need to know and train them continually.

Leadership

Leadership is defined as the ability to influence people and shape their behavior. Every company needs leadership. People in general are looking for leadership. There is great truth to the saying that leadership must come from the top, and nowhere is that more valid than in entre-preneurial companies. It is you, the entrepreneur, who must fill this role as the influencer of people and the shaper of behavior. After all, it was your vision that set the wheels in motion in the first place.

Leading as an entrepreneur means providing managerial, ethical, even spiritual guidance to those around you. Great leaders accomplish this through example, by practicing what they preach and using words only when necessary. Your work habits, your enthusiasm, your avail-ability, your communication style and your approach to managing con-flict all work together to set the cultural tone for your company and dictate not only the path to productivity, but also the level of produc-tivity the company achieves as well.

Perhaps most significantly, the leader sets the tone for company integrity. Every person you hire enters the company with a different degree of personal integrity. What was acceptable at an employee's pre-vious workplace may be sub-standard in yours. You as the leader owe it to yourself, your company and the people within it to clearly define and document acceptable codes of conduct. Everyone wants a company that works hard and whips the competition, but you also want a com-pany that wins while maintaining a high code of ethics and integrity. It is the entrepreneur who is responsible for creating and maintaining this culture. Not just through pep talks on ethics, but by putting systems and policies in place that guide the workplace in a direction of fairness with zero tolerance for unethical behavior.

This includes such systems as salary schedules, employee objectives, employee reviews, sexual harassment guidelines, strategic planning sys-tems, quality control initiatives, etc. These may seem like the problems and solutions of big companies, but you'll be surprised how often ethics issues arise in small, impassioned organizations. They can undermine your productivity faster than a computer virus, so it pays to be prepared.

Of course, taking time out to put such seemingly "unproductive" programs into place when you are neck deep in the all-consuming functions of product/service development, marketing and sales may seem like a waste of time. Nothing could be further from the truth. To achieve significant size, to last through the early business phase, your company will need an inspired work force. It doesn't take many breach-es in integrity to suck vital inspiration out of your company and leave it floundering.

Management by Objectives

Management is defined as the ability to influence people and shape their behavior by working with and through people to accomplish common goals. This definition is somewhat different than the one for leadership, because it includes others in the act of leading. Anytime you expect others to lead within the company, you'll need to make sure they are leading in the appropriate direction. It is your job as entrepreneur to manage the second-tier leaders by putting forth the objectives they must accomplish to help reach the company's common goal. In turn, it is the manager's responsibility to provide a documented list of objectives each employee must accomplish to contribute to the same goal.

Generally, each manager and each employee should have three to five objectives for the year. Include in the objectives a completion date and quantitative ways you will measure adequate performance. Studies show and experience holds true that when managers put forth clear goals and completion deadlines, employee performance increases dramatically.

Perhaps you're thinking there is a lot of emphasis being put on employee performance. That is the intent. Work force performance is the key to success and is therefore the primary indicator of an individual's contribution to the organization. Anything else is favoritism, and favoritism is a breach of integrity.

Objective Classes

Peter Drucker, in *Management: Tasks Responsibilities Practices* states that objectives have to be set in eight key aspects of your business:

1. Marketing
2. Innovation
3. Human organization
4. Financial resources
5. Physical resources
6. Productivity
7. Social responsibility
8. Profit requirements

The accumulation of your senior managers' objectives should include all eight areas and serve as the initial objectives for the company.

Consultative Management

So who sets these important objectives for managers and employees? Some supervisors feel they themselves should set the goals for their direct reports, but an enlightened view has management and the employees establishing the objectives together. Through this approach, objective setting becomes a give-and-take dialog to determine what the objectives should be and an exercise in establishing realistic expectation levels. Of course, you may be picturing meetings where the employees try to reduce the expectations of performance and minimize their workloads, but in practice the exact opposite is true. Employees actually tend to set higher goals for themselves. The manager's role most often is one of reducing the deliverables to more realistic levels. Companies that operate using this consultative management approach consistently outperform any company without goals or any company with mandated goals.

Management Training

Managers are not born, they are trained. You can hire experienced or inexperienced managers. Regardless, each manager should go through your company's management training program. During this program, managers will learn the company's policies and philosophies and review or learn for the first time results-oriented management techniques. They will also discover the importance and focus your company places on performance. A very basic curriculum would include:

- Company policies
- Fringe benefit plans
- Consultative management
- Management by objectives
- Strategic planning
- Quality control
- Departmental functions
- Marketing
- Sales
- Development
- Operations

- Accounting
- Management skills
- Interviewing
- Establishing objectives
- Coaching
- Employee reviews
- Leadership skills

With the rapid pace of business today, it's tempting to believe that the managers you will recruit won't need or have time for formal training. They will learn on the job. This is a dangerous attitude. Training is the time when you set management foundations and communicate the management culture of your company. It may take time in the present, but it will save you time—and money—in the future.

Integrity

Earlier in the chapter we stated that standards of integrity come from the top. This is true. It is also true that an employee's degree of integrity is difficult to judge before he or she becomes part of your organization. Previous employers are reluctant to level with you, and personal references will always give glowing reviews; otherwise they wouldn't be personal references. The risks are great. It only takes one person to throw off the delicate balance that exists within a well-performing work force.

You need all employees to be upstanding ambassadors of the company with both internal and external contacts. For example, filling out accurate expense reports, reporting to work regularly, giving credit when appropriate and generally working with others without hidden agendas or personal motives are crucial to a productive work environment.

You can tolerate mistakes, lack of knowledge and a host of other new employee shortcomings. They are expected and correctable. But what you cannot tolerate is a lack of integrity. If an employee is aware of your company's code of conduct, there is no reason to tolerate stealing, lying, misrepresentation or deliberate manipulation of others. The only appropriate action for this type of behavior is termination. Think of it as "tough love." It's doubtful you will be able to shock an employee with no integrity into having some. Termination is your best chance, and even if it doesn't wake up the problem employee, it will wake up everyone else.

In fact, why not stop the problem before it starts. Discuss the company's code of conduct during the interview process. That alone may weed out some of the undesirables before they infiltrate the company. The anguish you will save yourself and others in your organization will far outweigh the awkwardness of the discussion in an interview. If the candidate has the right stuff and is eager to work for you, he or she will admire you for it.

Employee Reductions

Watch CNBC too long, you start thinking like a CEO, and that's a dangerous thing. When you start admiring public company CEOs who make the tough decisions to take massive staff reductions and then follow with a comment from their CFOs relating to future cost savings, it's time to worry and stop watching financial news programs. This is so often the case. Both individuals during their interviews give the impression that they have accomplished some great objective. And Wall Street often buys into it by raising the stock a few points, albeit temporarily. Apparently, the analysts are watching too much CNBC, too!

In reality, the company that announces mass layoffs should see a reduction in their stock price, not an increase. After all, mass layoffs are neither indicators of intellectually gifted management, nor indicators of a company in good health. Mass layoffs are the result of poor planning, lackluster new products and ineffective management. Instead of seeing these teams as tough, efficient managers who make the hard decisions, look again. Instead of aspiring to be like them should the need ever arise, you should strive to rise above them.

To an employee, losing a job because of work force reduction is a humiliating experience. There's no better way to reinforce to the employees you let go that they really were nothing more than "head count." It sounds more like a stockyard than a company built on integrity, doesn't it? Imagine what the employees who stay are feeling and thinking. "Am I next?" "This company doesn't care." "I better start looking around for something else, we must be in trouble." One entrepreneur stated after a layoff at his six-year-old company that within six months, morale was so bad that all the eagles in the company took flight and all he was left with were the turkeys.

When you manage for results, you realize employees are the key to the success of the company. Employees who put their faith and their livelihoods—let's face it, their lives—in your hands deserve better leadership and management. They deserve leadership that looks around the corner to see and correct problems while they are small, rather than ignoring them, hoping they will all go away.

Phased Reductions

Sometimes, there is no choice. If a reduction in workforce becomes necessary, you should fire either the CEO or the CFO or both. Then begin an immediate program to:

- Freeze hiring
- Eliminate overtime and part-time hours
- Initiate cuts across the board. If an 8 percent cut is needed, start with 8 percent of the company's officers and work down
- Identify non-performers

Avoid the tendency to:

- Cut everyone's salary; now everyone is upset
- Cut all new employees; they haven't done anything wrong
- Eliminate marketing, a bad move unless they aren't generating leads
- Have the CFO wield the axe. If the department managers make the cuts, they will be less likely to overstaff.

Make sure you tell the terminated employees in person, not by mail or over the phone, of their employment status with the company. Let them know their release is not their fault, and set up an appropriate program to aid them in their search for new employment. These are some of the most difficult tasks of being an entrepreneur. They don't get any easier with practice. The best way to deal with them is to avoid them by building a successful, growing company.

Reviews of All Employees

Semi-annual and annual reviews are necessary for all employees, and the topic of discussion at each meeting is performance. At these times, you can candidly discuss one on one with the employees whether or not they are meeting their objectives and if their objectives need modification. It's also the time to map out specifically any corrective action so the employee knows exactly what he or she must do in the next 90 days to get back on track.

These are not fun discussions. You and your management team need to conduct them in a manner that is professional and non-argumentative. Both the employee's manager and the employee should exit with a clear understanding of the performance evaluation and the expectations going forward. Each employee is different. Some need a push, others need a big push. Some need to be challenged, others are challenging. For some, a few words of encouragement are all a manager needs to give. If you and your managers have taken the time to get to know the people in the company, you'll know the right motivation techniques. With new employees, there is nothing wrong with asking, one on one, the best way to motivate them.

Understand that each employee strives to achieve his or her own American dream. Each employee wants to succeed. This is basic to human nature. They want to contribute, and their goals in life are just the same as yours. For you to help them, you must put them in the right environment, surrounded by the appropriate tools and the Ten Entrepreneurial Success Strategies.

Partnerships and Multiple Decision Makers

Some companies are partnerships or have within the company itself multiple decision makers. In a consultative management environment such as this, even if there are multiple decision makers, someone must make the final decision for the company as well as for each department or functional area. You must hope that all the partners or decision makers are able to listen, guide the direction of decision discussions and decide who knows the most about the subject under review.

When you have multiple partners or managers who are not able to guide their areas in the same direction as the rest of the company, the result can be disastrous. Of course, decision makers should have their chances to voice their opinions and their rationale for them. After all the opinions are in, the company must choose its direction and move forward by documenting the initiative and communicating it to employees. Those partners and managers who attempt to take the company in a different direction will create chaos and make any significant productivity impossible.

> "We have seen the enemy, and he is us."
> —comic strip character, *Pogo*

One of the greatest multipliers to a small company's success is the consistency of its overall direction. When the partners and senior management spend their time focusing on marketing, sales and acquiring customers, the company is on the road to success. A cooperative management team that works with each other makes the team stronger than the individual members.

Sexual Harassment

No company is too small to face the devastating effects of a sexual harassment issue. Not only is sexual harassment against the law, it is morally wrong. There is no excuse for this type of behavior, which classically involves managers trading job assignments and raises for sexual favors. Sexual harassment can also include off-color jokes, pornography, inappropriate touching and a host of other behaviors that can result in very serious charges and lawsuits. In your corporate policy manual you must have a section relating to sexual harassment. Incidents left unresolved by management create serious performance issues throughout the company.

Attaining and Maintaining High Levels of Performance

Most growing companies will employ personnel with a wide range of backgrounds, work experiences and time on the job. In every company you'll have the high flyers who account for about 10 percent of your work force. Keep this group at all costs. Do everything possible to make them lifetime employees, and recognize it is their performance that lifts up the entire staff. Spend time with them; you'll learn a great deal. In every functional area they complete an inordinate amount of the work, are responsible for much of the innovation and naturally lead. This group can work anywhere. Keep them in your company, rather than driving them to your competitors.

Unfortunately, you also have a bottom 10 percent. These are the people who you need to replace. Others in the company tend to carry these people which is a wearying and thankless job for everyone involved. Inaction in matters of poor performance will result in a loss of the top performers, and the company can't afford that.

A young company that is going to grow and prosper must have everyone within it functioning productively. Just like the baseball team that makes mid-season trades, an entrepreneurial company has to constantly adjust to find the team that will win its way into the playoffs.

Management Responsibilities

All employees are not treated equally. Most young or entry-level employees believe the higher up the company ladder, the more money they make and the less work they have to do. They perceive that when they have paid their dues, they have earned the rewards that come with life at the top. Well, not so in an entrepreneurial company.

Actually, the reverse is true. High-level managers might earn more money, but with the position comes greater expectations of performance. Being a good manager is hard work and time consuming, and any first-time manager will have to go into overdrive and stay there to succeed.

Even above the managerial level, achieving the prestigious designation of company officer is even more demanding. The high-level visibility, the pressures of leading by example and the need to constantly increase productivity are overwhelming unless the individual is totally committed to the company. Outstanding officers constantly improve their teams, continually increase productivity and regularly train others. They can become inspirations for the entire company.

Responsibility for Your Team

In the military, commanders teach both officers and non-commissioned officers that the troops come first. The troops eat first, get paid first, are trained first. They are your team, and you are responsible for them.

When your employees become managers or officers in your company, they need to understand that same philosophy. The groups they are managing are their teams, and their responsibilities to those teams include:

▶ Planning

▶ Organizing

▶ Delegating

▶ Controlling

▶ Training

▶ Coaching

▶ Reviewing

▶ Increasing pay

In short, managers are responsible for everything it takes to improve the performance of their team. Sometimes managers must lead, and other times they must push. In either case, the expectation is higher performance.

Expect the Best

"One man can make a difference and everyone should try." Those are the words of John F. Kennedy. Of course today it's "one man or woman" who can make a difference. Regardless of the gender bias of the 1960s when this statement was made, its truth rings clear today. Each person has greatness within. By instilling the Ten Entrepreneurial Success Strategies, you will position every employee to become great and achieve their own American dream. After reviewing all the guidelines in this chapter, there are only two remaining tasks:

▶ Expect the best

▶ Convince each employee to expect the best from himself or herself.

Employees want to make a difference. They simply may have not yet found the environment in which they can shine. Everyone shines a little. You, the entrepreneur, just have to apply the polish.

All employees will work and think hard for a cause, and being the best company in your niche is a meaningful cause for everyone involved. Competitive success in the marketplace breeds pride and excitement for the company. Not arrogance, but pride, the kind that inspires employees with confidence and enables them to take on and complete tasks with enthusiasm. You believe in them, and they will believe in themselves.

Building a successful company isn't something that happens overnight; it's a journey. Former employees will be proud of their contributions, current employees will go to work everyday with a sense of excitement, knowing that when they look at the company they can say, "I helped create this!" They'll know their contributions meant something. Once you have fostered this feeling in your employees, you then will become a successful entrepreneur.

A Motivational Human Resources System

9

**Motivation comes from within,
And blossoms in a caring environment.
Take care of your employees,
And they will take care of you.**

Human Resources. Those words conjure up a number of images, few of which are very positive. Think about it. Some of our very first impressions of people in this profession paint terribly ugly pictures. A classic example is the holiday movie, *Miracle on 34th Street.* This is the charming story of a kind and caring old man who thinks he's Santa Claus and the chronically obsessive human resource psychologist who tries to prove that Kris Kringle is insane and ruin Christmas for all of New York. Of course, the psychologist's initial intentions were good. He's trying to protect Macy's, his employer, from potential law suits should the kindly Kris Kringle "lose control" while listening to the Christmas wishes of future Macy's shoppers. It's humorous, certainly, but the fact is that Hollywood has often portrayed personnel and human resource professionals as evil and anti-personal!

While certainly all human resource professionals are not like this Hollywood movie character, the stereotype came from somewhere and, more importantly, there is no reason in the world why you as the founder of your own company have to perpetuate this role. In fact, one thing Hollywood did accurately depict in the holiday classic is just how destructive poor human resources practices can be to a company and its image. So many companies say their employees are their most valuable assets, but few back up those words with behaviors.

Motivational Human Resources Systems are less about a department and more about a philosophy of bringing the best out in people. It's a belief that when people are achieving, the company and everyone associated with it is achieving, too. From this point forward, think of human resources as the systems that make people successful and therefore make the company successful. It starts with recruiting the right people, inspiring them, training them and putting the programs in place to evaluate and reward them.

Recruiting and Selecting Personnel

Many of the most important decisions you'll make involve evaluating and selecting employees for your company, particularly in the early stages. As we said before, employees represent you, they make first impressions for you, and they have the power to make a reality the dream you've worked so hard for up to this point. For most entrepreneurs, interviewing and hiring staff isn't a fun part of the job. Avoiding it is tempting. The mistake many entrepreneurs make is letting someone else do the work of hiring for them. While you don't necessarily need to do all the initial screening of applicants, you should be involved in the interviewing process and certainly in making the final decisions. It is the only way to ensure that the company's vision is being applied to the hiring decisions and that the people being interviewed can grow with the company.

Frequently, hiring decisions are pushed too far down the organizational chart. Before you realize it, the goal of having people who can grow with the company is gone. Managers tend to look for people who can accomplish tasks. That makes the managers' lives more productive. While task-oriented thinking is important for productivity, you're looking for people who can do the tasks plus a great deal more. You see the bigger picture and the possibilities for the candidate a few years down the line. The manager is unlikely to have this focus. The minute you begin hiring to fill a specific position, you begin your trek toward mediocrity.

Entrepreneurs don't necessarily need to screen resumes, but entrepreneurs should constantly be recruiting. Everywhere, everyday, a smart entrepreneur is on the prowl for top-quality people. Just because you're starting a company that makes software, for example, doesn't mean you won't find your next top sales representative in your favorite lunch spot. Recruiting today doesn't just happen through headhunters and personnel agencies. In fact, these are fairly uninspired, ineffective and expensive ways to find great people. The best way is to network through people you know. Ideally, you are looking for multiple applicants for each position. You can then use your company's selection process to determine which one is most likely to be able to handle the tasks and have a future in the organization.

There are numerous theories and techniques you can use to determine who is the best applicant out of a group of two or more. You may have seen them: various personality tests to show strengths and weaknesses, typical "interview" questions that indicate how well a person thinks under pressure, and many others. There are factors far more basic that you can use to quickly eliminate less desirable applicants. Elementary as the key hiring decision points below sound, they will help you make better decisions about people. As you read them, think about your best working environment and your worst. You'll see the connection between these factors and daily workplace reality. During and after an interview, ask yourself the following:

1. **Do you like the candidate?** Surprising as this sounds, liking the candidate is the single most important decision point. Let's face it, you will be spending 40 to 60 hours per week with this person. Will it be enjoyable or pure dread? Is this the person you want representing you to your customers and suppliers? Discovering how much you actually like the candidate is pretty easy. Just ask yourself if you had fun meeting and talking with this person during the interview.

2. **Is the candidate a mature individual?** You need people with a mature attitude about work, specifically a belief that advancement comes through effort and results, rather than longevity and presence. Too often employees feel they are owed pay raises, bonuses, even corner offices. They deserve more. These are all signs of immaturity, and immaturity's very presence in the workplace can undermine the productivity of not just the immature employee, but also everyone nearby. Mental maturity often reveals itself through home life. If a candidate has his or her home life in order, he or she is more likely to possess maturity.

Unless the candidate passes the likeability and the maturity tests, there's no point in going to the third test below. Eventually you will find a candidate who you really like and who has the maturity; in those instances, ask yourself the next question:

3.   **Will the candidate be able to handle the job?** For a candidate who is from outside your company, you'll need to make this determination after evaluating skills and experience. For a candidate who is a current employee, look at his or her performance in a current position. If an employee can't handle his or her first job, the likelihood of handling subsequent jobs is low. Furthermore, trying to reassign an employee who is under-performing in one position to another in the hope that they will improve is usually futile. You should only promote or reassign proven performers.

Inspiring People

Inspired employees are a requirement for entrepreneurial effectiveness. Without a group that is inspired daily and believes in the vision, the company won't go very far. Your daily tasks mount, and the hours in the day stay the same. It becomes apparent that you cannot do it all. You need people. You need inspired people.

In the workplace, inspiration comes from the top, but it must live within each employee. The spark that ignites the flame of inspiration is the passion that comes from working for a greater good. Employees who feel part of a cause are inspired to work harder and longer. People will "do" their jobs. People will "work" for a cause. Why? Because the work doesn't feel like work. It's exciting, and the employees feel as if they are making a difference, impacting the world. And they are. Your team will look to you to inspire them with words, actions and the work environment you create.

Inspiring your team is much easier if you have recruited effectively and if you are true to yourself. People with whom you mesh well will be more inclined to place their belief and trust in your ideas. Be aware that the job of inspirational leader brings with it very high expectations. If you are inspiring integrity, then you must display high integrity. If you are inspiring drive and motivation, then you must be driven and motivated. Living up to your words shouldn't be difficult if they represent who you truly are. It would be a tough act to keep up if it was counter to your being. You must be true to yourself when you inspire people. They can see through shallowness, and the very hint of it will uninspire them, diminish their trust in you and jeopardize your chances to succeed. Once the ideal is lost, it is very difficult to regain it.

Train Your Employees

When you hire someone, you and the new employee make an important commitment, one you both hope will last. The employee agrees to work for you. And the company agrees to pay the individual for his or her work plus provide training. That's right. You agree to invest in that employee and all the others so that they are able to perform, grow and succeed. Does on-the-job training count? Learn as you go? They count, but they alone are not enough for the employee or your organization if your goal is to achieve greatness.

Entrepreneurs know that their companies are rapidly changing. They know that their organizations will not be the same tomorrow as they are today. Every employee in the company has to continue to set the pace of change, not just keep up with it. Smart entrepreneurs know they are not going to get where they want to go with the same sets of skills that got them here today. It's going to take more. Training is the vehicle, and through it, employees should be worth significantly more to themselves and to you after three years. That is the mentality, and the training plan should reflect that. No successful entrepreneur would ever hire an individual without attempting to make that person better. You'll find it very difficult to compete otherwise.

Look around and ask yourself if your company has all talent and no results, superstars with no points on the board and few victories as a company. If so, those number one draft picks are ripe for some training. But what kind of training? Where do you begin? It starts with employee orientation and continues from there.

Employee Orientation

Employees, just like customers, need to have realistic expectation levels. Think about it, you have new employees with little or no real job experience, recent graduates from universities or high schools reporting for work. You may even have a few employees who are from other companies, the armed forces and technical schools. They all arrive with different expectations, none of them knowing how far from reality those expectations are. As the entrepreneur, it is your job to specifically define that reality and clarify expectations.

This defining and clarifying happens through employee orientation, which you or the next senior executive conducts within the first week of your new hires' employment. This does not have to be an elaborate dog-and-pony show. It is simply a meeting with all the new hires that defines reality and clarifies expectations for everyone. You may put the information into an orientation guide, but the booklet does not replace the physical training session.

A great way to start the meeting is to make sure everyone knows each other, and then specify the format for the meeting—that you welcome questions, that you'll have a question-and-answer period after each section you cover, etc.—so that everyone feels comfortable and understands the protocol. This is also your opportunity to demonstrate your leadership style and standards of authority. From a content perspective, at a minimum you'll want to cover the following areas:

Company Productivity

Discuss the expectations of employee productivity. It is important that all new employees understand that they are in a very competitive industry and the company can only succeed when each employee succeeds. The company requires high productivity from its employees.

Training

All employees need to understand the commitment the company is making to their growth and advancement. Training is a big part of that commitment. The reasons are simple. To achieve efficiency and function at peak performance, everyone must undergo an extensive training program that includes: company information, product or service training, industry education along with skill training for their specific areas of expertise. Like a chain, which is only as strong as the weakest link, the company is no stronger than the weakest employee. The training programs are designed to eliminate any weak links and provide a base of success for employees.

Attitude

There is no substitute for a great attitude, and all employees need to understand that maintaining a positive attitude is a job requirement. Work is not always easy, so sometimes this mandate is hard to fulfill. That doesn't matter. Behavior follows belief, so if you think positive, your actions will reflect that attitude before you know it. Behavior follows belief is an important concept as is the truth that a positive, enthusiastic attitude is contagious. By staying positive, you keep everyone else positive. If employees have problems at home, they are expected to leave them there. Personal problems not only distract the person involved, but they distract others the moment they are shared. If employees need to talk with someone, they should choose somewhere other than the workplace to do it, or seek the help of the personnel manager, an outside friend, a counselor, etc. Employees must realize that attitude will be very important to their success, not because the company only promotes positive people but because of human nature. Most successful people have very positive attitudes, and for that reason, others enjoy being associated and working with them. They naturally go further in life.

Meeting Expectations

Every employee should have a defined list of key objectives and a defined expected performance level. That objective-and-expectation list will vary for each employee depending on his or her functional position, the length of time in that position and the level of compensation. The company expects all employees to continually improve their performance and will evaluate individual progress every six months. It's a good idea to evaluate new employees even more often, perhaps quarterly, for the first year. The company and the employee together define the expected level of individual performance.

Career Growth

Help employees understand that career growth is a by-product of success. As the company grows and you grow professionally, careers can grow within the employees' areas of expertise and develop into various management positions. The company bases employees' growth and advancement on how well they perform their current tasks, their attitudes and their preparedness.

Proven Performers

Motivate your employees by letting them know that when new opportunities arise in the company, managers look within the company first and fill the positions whenever possible with existing employees who have a record of proven performance. Employees who are successful with their current tasks, in contrast to employees who are struggling, will most likely exceed performance expectations in new assignments.

Employee Turnover "Spring Drill"

Employees need to know from the start the concept of the spring drill. Although new employees are not expected to perform at the same level as five-year veterans, they will be evaluated at least once a year during the spring drill. At that time, the company implements planned labor reductions, evaluates its entire work force and ranks employees based on their individual performance and their delivery on expectations. Those individuals who are not meeting expectation (in the bottom 10 percent) will receive corrective training and a fair opportunity to improve performance—60 days, for example. If an employee does not meet the performance expectations after the 60 days, management will help them exit the company so they can find a career path where they can be more successful.

Working as a Team

Orientation is an ideal time to instill the belief in teamwork as a prerequisite for success. Everyone is expected to carry his or her load. When one person fails to do that, problems and dissention are inevitable. In team environments, peers will not tolerate behaviors like showing up late, leaving early, frequent absences or off-loading responsibilities onto others. Neither will managers, because this irresponsible behavior is counter to working as a team and tends to distract and upset others, which negatively affects productivity.

Nepotism

If you, the entrepreneur, have relatives working in the company, their performance must be outstanding, otherwise you and your relatives will be accused of nepotism. There is nothing more foolish than causing a good employee to leave because of favoritism toward relatives. Employees need to know that there are no favorites and no favoritism at your company. Advancement is based on performance.

Sexual Harassment

Sexual harassment is a serious offense. During orientation, employees need to realize the gravity of this issue and understand that any violation of the company's sexual harassment policy will result in immediate termination.

Compensation Philosophy

Compensation is usually not an issue, unless your pay scale is below the market average. If it's too low, you will know about it because key employees will leave and mass exodus could occur. If your pay scale is too low, meaning below industry averages, you have a serious problem.

A good goal for wages is somewhere close to the 75 percentile with bonus plans for outstanding performance.

You cannot afford to lose your best people for any reason; therefore, it pays to pay people what they are worth. Typically, the higher the compensation, the lower the attrition rate, all things being equal between you and the other possible employers. Of course, everything is never equal. You will have some attrition if you hire outstanding people because they are in demand.

During orientation, make sure employees know and understand that your compensation plan includes additional compensation based upon the achievement of definable performance. A base scale in the 75 percentile, with bonus performance equal to 50 to 75 percent of the base is one example. If you can afford it, this will usually provide a stable, motivated work force.

Salary Schedules

During orientation, you need to introduce the concept of salary schedules and define yours. A basic salary schedule will show salary levels by function, and each function could have several steps or grades based on the level of experience. Raises and advancements are tied to performance and the achievement of experience levels. Salary schedules provide full disclosure of employees' earnings potential in their current positions. Employees can review their own salary schedule with their managers, but reviewing this topic generally during orientation sets the tone of fairness and full disclosure. Employees can see their own growth paths and perhaps even set a few financial goals they can work hard to attain. Just as important, salary schedules promote fairness in your system and help you avoid accusations of discrimination or favoritism. Being accused of either of these two crimes will kill any team's chances of achieving high productivity.

Benefits

Your benefit plan needs to be competitive with the plans of other employers in your area, and during orientation all employees will learn of the specifics. You do not have to match the benefit plans of GM or IBM, but you will want to make up for the differences in other ways. Companies today are doing this very creatively by offering everything from sports tickets to educational scholarships, and in the process are enticing people away from companies that are less inspired.

Stock Options and Stock Purchase Plans

These are in the news constantly, so employees will want to know the details of your plan. Orientation is a great place to teach the specifics, the most important of which is that stock options at your company do not replace fair compensation and benefits. Nothing drains the productivity of a company faster than a work force living and dying by the number and value of stock shares owned and optioned. Of course you want to make sure that the people who contributed to the success of the company can share in the fruits of that hard work, but you also want them to be fairly compensated along the way. It's all part of the commitment, and it results in a hard working, highly focused work force. People will work hard if they feel they are being treated fairly. They will work even harder when they own a piece of the dream.

Integrity

We've talked about integrity a great deal so far in this book. And here it is again, a subject that you'll need to discuss in detail with the employees at orientation. The company's integrity level is the mirror image of the entrepreneur and his or her executive management. If there is more than one person guiding the company's integrity, the people and the message must be unified so there is no confusion and the information is actionable. Make sure employees realize that the company sets its own standard of integrity, not the employees. Regardless of the level of integrity the employees have, which is very difficult thing to gauge in an interview, you expect them to live up to the company's standard. How do you establish a baseline acceptable level for integrity? You sit down and define the company's code of ethical conduct. Ethics can vary by industry, but truthfulness, honesty, taking responsibility, and giving credit to others are all universal traits of integrity. Set your integrity levels high; anything else will lead to wasted opportunity.

Human resources is about the human side of running a business. Experience proves true that the ultimate success of any entrepreneur is a function of how well he or she recruits, trains, re-trains and retains a work force base. It plays a huge role in dispelling the myth that entrepreneurs can't run their own businesses. You can have a team of committed, enthusiastic employees ready to work extended hours, yet completely incompetent without the proper training. You can also have the most well trained, knowledgeable employees who produce little and leave quickly because they are uninspired or underpaid. These factors make the difference between entrepreneurs who achieve initial success and then fail or stall and those who have initial success and continue to grow.

If you lead your team with integrity, train them better than your competition trains their employees, then you will win most of the time. Even if the other side has people who are smarter, higher paid or better educated, none of that matters. If they can't play as well as you do, you win. Not once in awhile, but most of the time.

A Resource-Oriented Accounting System

10

Financial strength is a mark of leadership.
Fiscal impact should direct priorities.
Establish cash flow as keeper of the flame,
And watch your company flourish.

We all have our image of accountants. They are stereotypically the company bean counters, the people who count every penny and remind department managers just how much money they don't have to spend. Or, if you are a fan of the *Dilbert* comic strip by Scott Adams, accountants are trolls who live in the building basement and spend their days erasing budget numbers. That is until Dilbert himself, who was sentenced to work in the accounting department, erases the accounting department budget, and all the trolls, i.e., accountants, vanish into thin air! A perfect utopian dream for a project manager!

Accountants have a bad image, and perhaps in some companies they have worked hard to earn it. In your entrepreneurial firm, the accounting department is no longer the department that says, "No." It's the department that works with you to figure out solutions and create opportunities. The day you dedicate yourself to establishing a Resource-Oriented Accounting System is the day the accounting department and your company are liberated and given the wings to grow the right way. The accounting department will not be locked away in the basement of the building or even the corner of it. It will be integrated and involved in all areas to enhance the decision making process.

Accounting departments are a resource to all departments, as opposed to being simply the natural enemy of marketing and sales.

Decisions affecting corporate financial performance, such as marketing programs, product pricing, acquisitions or licensing agreements are a few of the items that can have severe unintended consequences to the company's profitability. People who think in terms of numbers can foresee and eliminate potentially disastrous surprises by being involved early in the decision process rather than afterwards when the primary job is cleaning up the mess.

You need to know right now that many of your employees (probably most) will not like the idea of accounting being involved in the decision making process. Eventually, however, your employees will begin to understand that it is accounting's job to help train them in fiscal matters rather than criticize. They will establish trust, which once formed, is the basis for an accounting team that can become the keystone of a fiscally oriented organization. Until accounting becomes a resource for the rest of the company, they are nothing more than bean counters, a task anyone can do.

Accounting's involvement will not come naturally, because accountants have very little experience reaching out to others in a company. It is accounting that must take the first step and several steps afterwards to get the ball rolling. By offering assistance in budgeting, pricing, estimating, establishing compensation plans, anything that involves dollars, and focusing on one department specifically, accounting will establish a precedent of assisting and teaching. They will make people's lives easier, not harder, and the rest of the company will follow.

Keep in mind that accounting as a resource can only happen if your accounting department has the highest level of ethics, a prerequisite for trust. Trust is critical to gaining widespread acceptance of this accounting system model.

Accounting Ethics

Integrity and ethics are critical in every aspect of your business, but if they are not present in the accounting department, the repercussions can be devastating. For example, you should never find yourself defending the integrity of your company's financial reports. Your accounting department must follow accounting standards and the FASB (Federal Accounting Standards Board) rules explicitly. Companies, even large ones, get into trouble by misreporting numbers related to revenue recognition, expense reporting, and amortization and depreciation.

Not only will the employees lose faith and trust due to ethical violations, any issues regarding the integrity of the financial reports will cause a serious loss of confidence by investors and customers as well. Why companies would even attempt to manipulate revenue numbers is beyond comprehension. Yet more than one company has embarked upon this fool's path to cover up poor performance in a reporting period and by so doing destroyed the very company they were trying to protect. Ethics means that accounting departments report the facts, take the heat if the numbers are bad and get on with it. Under no circumstances should accounting alter the financial results.

With the importance of ethics clearly out in the open, the remainder of this chapter will show how accounting can integrate into your company and provide assistance in a number of important areas, particularly acquisitions.

Setting Standards

Ethics is also about accuracy and attention to detail. Entrepreneurs should set accounting standards that minimize errors and duplication of effort. For example, all the accounting systems, including accounts payable, payroll, general ledger, billing, accounts receivable, prospect and customer databases and electronic mail should use information processing from day one. These systems are not expensive, and the right vendors can make sure they are trouble free. You can even look for other integrated, specialized applications for your specific industry. Very seldom, if at all, will you need custom-developed software. Further, applications that employees use through the company should be web-based for ease of accessibility. You'll be amazed at the improvement in productivity once accounting takes an aggressive stance toward the installation of all applications.

Financial Planning and Budgeting

Financial planning and budgeting are natural functions of accounting, but under this resource-oriented system, they are more of a collaborative exercise rather than an individual endeavor. Each one of your department managers should be involved in his or her department's budgeting process. This is a learning experience for managers and a golden opportunity for each of them to discover everything necessary to take over control of their areas and be fiscally responsible.

The primary planning documents will be the standard accounting reports:

‣ Balance sheet

‣ Profit & loss statement

‣ General ledger

In addition, other reports such as capital additions and cash flow analysis will be important.

Cash flow analysis is a particularly valuable report that every entrepreneur needs to see on a regular basis. Financial reports are for investors, the management team and a long-term view. Cash flow analysis, by contrast, shows exactly the cash flow picture today. How many months of operation are left without increases in sales? A different version shows the yearly sales estimate and the cash gain or loss for the year. These are important indicators of the health of your company. It's very easy to have a fast-growing, profitable business run out of cash. It happens for one or more of several reasons:

‣ The company purchased, rather than leased, too many assets.

‣ The company grew too fast.

‣ The company lost focus and initiated too many start-up projects.

‣ The company had insufficient working capital.

The last of these reasons is an interesting problem. It can be devastating if your company isn't profitable, or no problem at all if you have a business that is growing fast and is profitable. Raising additional equity under the latter circumstance is very easy. This is a great problem to have and a fun one to solve.

Sales Contracts and Administration

Your sales department will need to review sales contracts with the accounting department. Although many or most of your agreements will come in without changes, some will have substantial changes. Occasionally, someone will try to rewrite your entire contract. Avoid doing this and use addendums to modify the agreement. One contract with addendums is easier to administer than custom contracts for each customer. Accounting can serve the sales department by providing a quick 24-hour turnaround of contract issues. Speed is synonymous with customer satisfaction and is critical to the success of your sales effort.

Sales Contract Penalties

A good business relationship needs to be a win for both the buyer and seller. It takes a partnership, two parties working together to create performance.

Occasionally a customer will request or demand some type of financial penalty for non-performance or missing a target deadline. Sales contract penalties create an adversarial relationship from the beginning, and it's difficult to establish a partnership unless a positive attitude exists. Avoid penalty clauses and substitute with win-win type contracts that reward both the buyer and the seller for performance above the norm.

Keep in mind that most customers who insist on penalty clauses in contracts plan to collect those penalties. Maybe you do not need them as customers.

Licensing of Resale Products

Sometimes you will need to license a product for inclusion in your product or service. Accounting can help by working with you to determine the terms of the licensing agreement. Large and well-established companies document quite clearly your alternatives. When working with smaller companies like your own, however, you need to be careful. Let accounting help you determine how much you can pay. Then protect yourself against the failure of the small company. Should the company go under, penalty clauses will not help you. You and the accounting department should set up a type of escrow agreement for product plans or software code. An escrow agreement provides for system documentation, either software or engineering plans, to be sent to an escrow agent and released to the customer in the event of bankruptcy.

Without a doubt, you want your small company partners to stay in business. The tendency with young companies is to negotiate too tough with these small players. Do just the opposite. Make the licensing agreement a win-win, where you save money and the supplier makes a reasonable return. Small vendors are not any help to you if they are suddenly bankrupt because the sharp deal you negotiated was too tough. Battle with the big vendors, and protect the small ones.

Acquisitions

Acquisitions are vitally important to the growth of your company; yet there is no box on any organizational chart where these duties rest. The role accounting plays in acquiring a company is massive. That's why you're reading about the subject in this section of the book. If your accounting department isn't able to handle acquisitions, your company will be at a severe competitive disadvantage and find it very challenging to grow.

Frequently, the CEO and entrepreneur will be the acquisition experts, sometimes it's business development, and often it's handled by the CFO. Wherever you place the driving force for acquisition, until you involve the accounting department your acquisition will be flawed by over payment.

The best acquisition initiatives will be a joint effort between the CEO or entrepreneur, business development and accounting, but there are a few prerequisites. First, you should pursue acquisitions on a planned and focused basis rather than an opportunistic one. Looking at everything that comes through the door is a recipe for disaster. Focus is the key. Second, you are ready for an acquisition program only after you have your strategic plan in place. The plan should identify your company's opportunities and weaknesses. You'll clearly see any opportunities for new products, services or geographical expansion.

The acquisition group, using the strategic plan as a starting point, will define the types of acquisitions required. After they identify the target business types, the team begins the acquisition process based on the following acquisition program implementation procedure:

Select Acquisition Agent or Broker

Find a company or consulting group that specializes in acquisitions in your selected industry and the markets you serve. It is essential that the firm you select has good market research capability and existing industry databases. They will be able to derive market research from existing files rather than searching the industry. If you find the right acquisition professional, he or she can get you the answers you are looking for almost immediately. This is a time and money saver.

Initiate Market Research

Your acquisition group has identified the market areas in which you'll most likely find the type of company you want to acquire. From here your acquisition firm will perform a market research study to compile a list of specific target companies in the specific market.

Screen Candidates

You may find 30 or more possible businesses in the search. A simple screening by the acquisition team leader could narrow the group to the eight or ten that look appealing. Screening can be based on size, market share, geographical representation, profitability, as well as other variables.

Establish Phone Contact

You need to establish contact with the CEOs of the target companies. The best method is a direct contact, a simple discussion about the possibility of some type of joint relationship. Many acquisition searches end up as joint ventures, licensing agreements or product acquisitions, and that's perfectly fine. A good goal for the first call is an agreement to exchange information about your company and theirs.

Initial Visits

After you and the target companies exchange information, you'll quickly discover which of the candidates are viable options that match your specifications. Your next step is to visit the top three or four candidates and make personal observations. Be prepared to describe your company's position and vision. On this first visit, you may feel free to discuss the possibility of an acquisition. If there is any interest, you should both agree to exchange financial reports.

Preparing an Offer

If after your initial visits you have one or more viable candidates, you need to create an offer. This is where accounting plays an important role in this process. If you have two candidates, either of which would fulfill your needs, you will have significant negotiating leverage. Accounting should structure the offer, review the target company's financials and create a pro forma. This is a combination of your company's financial statements and the candidate's financial statements. A pro forma will show the anticipated value of the combined entities. The hard part is coming to a realistic value, a number that will make a return of capital possible and increase your growth and earnings. There are several non-perfect formulas for determining value. Your best method is to use several and obtain a range, from which you select your offer point and establish your upper limit. A few of those formulas are:

- **Multiple of cash flow.** Many firms are sold for four to eight times EBITDA (earnings before interest, taxes, depreciation and amortization less debt)

- **Multiple of sales.** This is used in some industries where sales revenues are easily converted to other companies. By itself, this formula can be very misleading.

- **Multiple of earnings.** This works only after the acquisition candidate's financial statements have been modified to be identical to yours.

- **Value of assets.** If the acquisition is a product-oriented decision, a replacement cost must be determined for the product or products being acquired.

- **Industry norms.** Each industry has a usual and customary method of assigning value. Use this method, but also use the others as a check.

- **The real factor.** How does this acquisition increase sales and earnings for the acquiring company? You may make the best deal of all time, but unless it shows up in your sales and profitability, what good is it?

Do not spend time looking for a magic formula for the right price; there isn't one. Buying a small company is an art rather than a science. What a business is worth is different than what it will take to buy the business.

Presenting the Offer

When you present the offer, do it at your office, and be prepared for a wide range of responses. During the previous meetings and phone calls you should have had some discussions regarding valuation. However, if you're the first to present a specific valuation, get ready, the responses can be "You're a few thousand below our target" to "You're ten times lower than our valuation" to someone abruptly standing up and walking out.

Entrepreneurs will frequently see value in their own companies that doesn't exist. When you find someone who is receptive to your offering, (and some who initially react negatively will eventually come around), even though you might be as much as 25 percent to 50 percent apart, you will usually be able to get together. Questions you need to ask yourself and your team include: Does the deal make sense? Is it best for both companies? Will the acquisition cause revenue and earnings to grow faster?

Letter of Intent

If you reach an agreement on price, the next step is to prepare a letter of intent. The letter should cover at a minimum:

- **Terms.** How much your company will pay and when the payments are due
- **Clear definition of earn-outs.** Part of the amount to be paid can be subject to future performance
- **Review of due-diligence steps.** A review of all aspects of the business
- **Preparation of a definitive agreement.** A comprehensive, attorney prepared purchase agreement showing all terms, conditions and warranties
- **Plus anything else you have negotiated.**

Due Diligence

Due diligence is a thorough review of all aspects of the business. An important rule in acquisitions is stop if anything occurs that makes you suspect the seller's integrity. Do not proceed with the deal. Granted, you can make contractual agreements to protect yourself, sometimes, but if the seller is intent on misrepresentation, you will not find everything. The items you and your team should review or analyze include:

- An audit of the balance sheet
- An assessment of the accuracy of the profit & loss statement
- A review of the payroll records
- A review of accounts payable records
- A discussion of all outstanding receivables with the customers
- A verification of company performance with customers (all items involving customers may need to be accomplished with an independent auditor)
- A review of attrition records for customers, employees
- An interview with management and key employees
- An understand of their billing cycle. (Is it the same as yours? Is revenue spilling over from one accounting period into the next?)

- An analysis of product stability and the kind of maintenance required for each product
- An evaluation of all disclosed liabilities
- A determination of the scope of undisclosed liabilities, unfulfilled customer commitments, possible customer or employee suits

Post-Acquisition Integration Plan

Before you sign any definite agreement, your team and the acquisition candidate's team must agree on the integration plan. Arriving at the agreement before the deal is final will keep the post-acquisition trauma to a minimum, which is critical to maintain productivity. By working through the details before the deal is complete, you will save endless hours of negotiation during a very critical time—the days immediately following the acquisition close. Some of the items to resolve include:

- Accounting system and chart of accounts
- Fringe benefit plans
- Compensation plans
- Products to be eliminated
- Personnel changes
- Levels of authority
- Communications plan

You, the entrepreneur, need to be very specific; this will be a real test of your integrity. If you know that you will terminate certain people after the acquisition, you must disclose this to the sellers. Buying a company and then making a host of undisclosed changes is not worth the grief and hard feelings it will create. Be true to the company you are buying, and in the process, you will be true to yourself.

The Definitive Agreement

Your lawyer will convert the letter of intent plus the items from your due diligence into a comprehensive agreement called the Definitive Agreement. Take responsibility for negotiating this agreement with the seller; do not turn this process over to the lawyers unless you want the fees and the deal to get out of control.

The best lawyers will tell you to stay involved. The principals can quickly agree on issues, and the lawyers can document the agreements.

When lawyers negotiate the issues, anything can happen. You want your team in control.

Tax Consequences

The form of purchase must take tax issues into consideration. Due to the rapidly changing tax laws and the complexity of existing laws, expert tax help is essential. Frequently, tax issues will adversely affect one or both parties. Instead, it should be a win-win for both groups. If the seller and his or her employees end up with unexpected tax consequences, you will have a new group of employees who are not bringing with them very positive attitudes. Work through their issues, as well as your own, in advance.

The tax-favored purchase is to buy assets as opposed to private stock. When buying assets you actually are buying the business, all assets and liabilities, everything except contingent and undisclosed liabilities. Granted, in a stock purchase, you can protect yourself through indemnification clauses, but they offer little comfort when the lawsuit is greater than the seller's net worth.

If the company is public, you'll be buying stock, but you'll also have better records and a more complete history to review.

Closing and Integration

Close quickly and implement your integration plan immediately. It's important to make the agreed-upon changes in all areas soon after closing. If there is a lag between closing and taking control, take as many integration steps as possible prior to closing.

This sets a new tone and lets everyone know who is in charge. Do not overdo the effort and destroy a fine company that you have just purchased. If you acquired the company with the understanding they would stay separate, then your integration efforts will revolve around accounting and employee benefit issues. If you acquired it with the view of being completely integrated, then sooner is better than later.

A Resource-Oriented Accounting System will be the foundation of a fiscally sound company. All managers will be brought into fiscal planning, and all transactions will be evaluated from a fiscal perspective. Fiscal strength will increase, and the result will be greater profitability and growth.

A Zero Defects Product Development Program

11

The basic core strength of any entity is its product.
Only designers and craftsmen make a great product.
These quiet, driven men and women strive to create;
They turn our dreams and visions into reality.

Everyone has his or her list of great American products. These four will likely be included in the ranks of many of them:

- **The Clipper Ship.** One of the greatest products of all time, this well-conceived, majestic design was built by Yankee craftsmen. These ships sailed so well, they kept the steam engine off the oceans for over 40 years.

- **The IBM 1403 Printer.** More than any other single component, this printer thrust IBM computers in the 1960s to the forefront of the business computing world. Running at 600 lines per minute in a time when everyone else had devices that were measured in characters per minute astonished all competitors. They sold like popcorn balls and devastated the competition.

- **Microsoft Windows.** This product unleashed the power of computing to all the non-technical users. Everyone became computer literate, and everyone could make a computer work. It was easy to use, fast, intuitive and became a model for all new user software products.

- **Your product.** All you have to do is build it! Perhaps building one of the all-time best products seems like an overly ambitious goal. But why not aim high? The next great product will be invented by someone; it may as well be you.

Before you start, spend a few moments reading the following pages and learn about the problem of defects. You'll discover just why Zero Defects Product Development is one of the most critical endeavors for your new company.

In most boardrooms, hearing the words "product" and "defect" uttered in the same sentence is enough to send a wave of fear through even the most confident of executives. Product defects are serious business problems that have the power to, at the very least, ruin a company's reputation and possibly shut down a business forever.

Some cases of defective products are more public than others. Corning's silicone breast implants, Firestone tires, the Sulzer hip replacement device and many others are all product-defect issues that landed unrelenting front-page headlines with devastating results for the companies. However, a product defect doesn't have to land on the front page of the *New York Times* to destroy a company. In fact, if the only people who know about a product's problem are your customers and your potential customers, you are finished. Consider the technology company that released software with a rogue computer virus embedded in every diskette because they didn't have time to check the quality *and* make their quarterly numbers. The resulting recall process was financially devastating, image depleting and personally embarrassing.

In case you do not yet have the proper perspective on the gravity of product defects, a simple Internet search using a popular search engine for the words "product defect" yields over half a million results; other search engines' results are similar. A random sample of the pages revealed well over 75 percent of the listings viewed were for attorneys' web pages specializing in wrongful death, personal injury and professional malpractice related to defective products! There are legions of people who are "aggressively pursuing" product-defect cases, and many are looking for class-action lawsuits with big dollar settlements or damage awards. And if your company is producing any products for children, read this chapter every day and live by it.

A defective product will harm you and your new company by either destroying your reputation or by running you into bankruptcy with legal fees and damages. The best protection you have is to put into place your own *aggressive* program, such as a Zero Defects Product Development Program, which stops defect problems before they start.

Zero defects sounds like a pie-in-the-sky dream, especially in an age when products are so complex. Aren't software bugs a part of the feature set? The reality is that consumers are not very accepting of defects in products, and even software bugs are becoming increasingly unacceptable. Zero Defects Product Development means just that: develop products (and services) with a zero tolerance for malfunction. It isn't easy, but it's what you're paying your development team members to do.

What Zero Defects Requires

Every area of your new business requires talent, experience and a strong customer focus. Nowhere is this more critical than in the development of new products, particularly for a start-up or entrepreneurial firm. Every single person in your organization needs to realize that if the products or services do not have a solid base built on quality, your days as a business are numbered. No amount of marketing or sales talent will make the company successful long term if the products or services are inadequate. Products or services must deliver on promises, and that takes a talented development team that can turn wishes into reality.

Zero Defects Product Development also takes a great deal of experience. Find people to lead your development efforts who have made their mistakes and learned how to avoid the same traps. Of course, there will always be trial and error, but using your capital and your customers to establish a development learning curve is very dangerous. The truth is, your base product line or service must be solid enough to carry your company through its start-up phase. More than one company has risen rapidly and then flamed out because its first product or service attempt did not perform adequately for its early customers.

You don't get a second chance to make a first impression, as the saying goes, so it's important that your first product be well conceived from the customer's perspective. For products, this can be anything: the way it feels in your hand, how it works, its durability, its reliability and more. For services, well conceived relates to how the service is delivered, the value for the price, the ease in which the service is rendered, things that take the "hassle factor" out of the customer experience. Take software, for example. Well-conceived software must be designed to minimize down time due to software bugs. Developers will work hard to accomplish this criterion, and when they are done, if the software works perfectly, the development team may feel they have achieved success. Not so. When it comes to software, customers expect it to work and be easy to use. Without achieving this ease-of-use component, the development team will have failed.

And that leads to the customer focus. Good development teams think like customers. They have an ability to remain objective about the project even though they are living and breathing it ten or more hours a day. The minute they begin thinking like engineers, designers or consultants they have lost the customer focus. Rather, they need to remain true to usability, simplicity of operation, customizability, response time and reliability. For services, a customer focus revolves around ease of implementation, customizability, personal attention and follow through. Can you accomplish these expectations? Only if you are serious about succeeding.

Garbage In, Garbage Out

Nearly all product or service development endeavors involve purchasing or licensing products or services from other vendors. Dell, for example, buys parts and licenses software from hundreds of vendors and assembles them into computers. Homebuilders hire carpenters, stone masons and drywall contractors to build a house. Very few products and services are produced on an island with no help from the outside world. That puts your company in a precarious position. Your product is only as good as the products and services that go into it. Regardless of whether we are talking about licensing a software module, buying a microprocessor or subcontracting with a stone mason for a home-building project, remember these rules:

- **Rule Number One.** Everything does not perform as advertised or represented. Many companies are famous for selling futures. Sales people forget what is real (deliverable) and what is imaginary (undeliverable). Some providers are trained to say, "Yes" and figure out the details of "how" later. Sometimes they never do.

- **Rule Number Two.** Every time you buy or license a product or sub-contract a service, read Rule Number One.

Every product or service purchased and incorporated into your customer offering will impact customer satisfaction and be a direct reflection on you, your reputation and your company. If garbage goes in, garbage will come out, and that's a guarantee. The problem is that you never know if the expensive component you just bought is garbage.

Eliminate a lot of headaches by never assuming a product or service will perform as represented in the sales literature or by a sales representative. Before anything goes into the product or service design, conduct quality-assurance tests. If the vendor isn't willing or wants all the funds in advance, consider this a caution flag.

On occasion, you may think you are safe. After all, the company selling the product or service seems great and has a great reputation. The company may even be on the Fortune 500. It's tempting, but reputation is not enough. Don't assume the product or service will deliver just because:

- **You're buying from a reputable vendor.** Most vendors have some sub-standard products or services.

- **Several hundred people use this product or service.** Their requirements and environments are different.

- **Numerous references gave their seals of approval.** They may be justifying their own purchase decisions.

- **Your in-law recommends it.** There may be hidden agendas. (Use extra caution for former in-laws.)

- **The vendor answers questions about capability by saying, "You can do that."** Translated "you" the buyer, means the company has no intention of adding that capability.

- **Someone is trying to sell you a sophisticated, high-tech product.** Always be wary.

Quality-checking the products and services that go into your company's product and service offerings is imperative to the zero-defects model. If your final product is flawed because of outside vendors, you have a right to be disappointed but no real recourse with the vendor. The problem rests in entrepreneurial naiveté. Now you know. Before purchasing, licensing or contracting any goods or services, successfully complete the quality-assurance tests.

The Most Important Project

Developing a product or service is the most important project you'll undertake as a young company. The success or failure of the project can directly impact the success or failure of the company through this relationship: a successfully designed product gives you a shot but doesn't guarantee market success; a failing product can waste your shot and guarantee market failure. Adherence to a process that puts all the steps into logical order, complete with built-in checks and balances, is critical to the development of a successful product or service.

The bulk of this chapter will focus on product, rather than service development. The last portion of the chapter will center on the special considerations of service development. Much of the development process is the same for both products and services. Frequently companies will take products and turn them into services through unique marketing and pricing strategies. For example, many hardware and software companies will price their products on a monthly basis to generate recurring revenue. They have effectively converted a product into a service. Other companies provide consulting or implementation services around a product offering. The company will assess the customer's needs and deploy the software or hardware solution over the course of months or even years.

Sometimes it is hard to delineate between products and services, but the key to building a strong, product-oriented company is to build products and turn them into services. Conversely, the key to building a valuable service-oriented company is to productize your services. Either way you look at it, the sections in this chapter are of value to anyone developing a product or a service and, most likely, both.

The Zero Defects Development Program—Products

IBM used this process during the 1960s for their 360 product line and its related software systems. The specific outline covered in this chapter is the result of 40 years of technological improvements both in hardware and software and a great deal of trial and error. Although it is based on the development of information technology products, it represents a modern blueprint of how to build anything. There are six phases, and each one assumes that you and your team have completed the one before it successfully. By following these six steps with a high degree of integrity, your team will produce a high-quality product with zero defects.

Phase 1—Conception

If this phase is done correctly, your product is off to a great start. You'll also save yourself a lot of money and time. It is worth the time and effort to think through a project, and this one is no exception. When you and your team are dreaming up a fantastic product, be sure to bring the euphoria back down to earth by focusing on these important elements:

- **Product Concept.** Ask yourself what you intend the product to do, what is the scope of this product and the size of effort to make it a reality. For a software product, ask how may different page or screen views you'll need and the number of interactive and batch processes, and begin rough schematics of all screens and reports. For hardware, envision the control pad, the footprint of the device, the moveable parts and the basic method of operation.

- **Market Analysis.** You will have completed much of this work when preparing your business plan, but now is a great time to review it, making sure nothing has dramatically shifted in the market. Take a new look at both the actual and potential market sizes. Is the market new, emerging or mature? Who are the competitors? Is the market a small niche, or will the size attract IBM and Microsoft? What is the probability of a new entrant being successful—either your company or others? What are the barriers to entry?

- **Business Analysis.** Again, you should have completed this analysis in the business plan, but you probably have more knowledge and insight at this point, so your analysis may need modification. Analyze the total business and how it will look. How much of the product do you see being installed or purchased? What resources will you need to install and support the purchased products? Is the installation of the product fast and easy to replicate, or is it complex, requiring a great deal of custom analysis and tweaking? If the product is in the information technology realm, will it need to support multiple operating systems and databases? Will this product interface with the clients' existing systems? Can this product support a real business, including yours and the people to whom you intend to sell the product?

- **Return on Investment.** A business is a hobby, unless it is actually generating a monetary return on investment. You should now have enough information to get a rough estimate of your expected return on the efforts to build your product. In performing this analysis, you must take into account the size of your market, which is the amount of money spent if everyone bought what you are selling and how much it costs you to make your product. By selling to a fraction of your market, you must be able to cover your costs.

The size of the market and the cost of the product-build must make sense. In some markets, securing a 20 percent share can be very good. But if it does not cover your costs, then the business will not generate a return. In other markets, a 2 percent share may cover the costs and bring in a wealth of revenue. Finally in niche markets, a company may need to capture 60 percent market share to see a return on investment. The business aspect of development really hits home with the return-on-investment analysis. You'll quickly find that the development process at this point is a series of choices about opportunity, necessity, setting priorities and evaluating potential. Knowing which products have the best return and working on those first will help create a healthy company with the resources to keep growing.

Phase II—System Design

At this phase, you and your team will determine exactly how your new product will deliver on its promises. You'll study each system in detail and map out a design plan.

- **User Interfaces.** We live in an information age, and regardless of what kind of product you are designing, chances are it will contain or use some type of electronic components. Those components will not only be interfacing with humans but also with other computer systems. In fact, any sophisticated product will usually require interfacing with one or more existing systems. At this point in the system design, you and your team need to determine what kinds of environments exist and within which environments your product will function.

  By environments we mean the different networking software, protocols, operating systems, and databases. Look at the typical environments of your market to determine how the product will fit in and how users will actually use it. Will it be via a personal computer, a stand-alone appliance, a hand-held device, a cell phone or even a unique device that's never before been seen. Without exception, the product should be as turn key as possible, requiring little customer effort to get it installed and running. If the product takes great effort to install and operate, your company will need to provide that level of support. Otherwise you risk slow sales, dissatisfied customers or a product that never fulfills its true potential.

- **Technical Design.** So often when it comes to technical design, engineers want to do it all from scratch. This is not the time to spend limited resources proving you can build a better Microsoft Windows. Rule Number One: Don't reinvent the wheel. If the hardware or software exists and it passes your quality test, use it. Rule Number Two: If you find a need to write system software, database managers, screen handlers, operating systems or anything else that has been working successfully for years, go back and read Rule Number One. This should sound familiar.

  Using standard, quality products doesn't just save you time and money, they can actually provide a level of perceived quality that adds marketing value. Look for products that are scalable to your needs with high functionality and a solid reputation at a good price. Avoid using unproven operating systems, programming languages or database managers. You will always have a few main choices and several second-tier choices for your system design. There is too much at risk not to select from your main choices. Most of the second-tier choices won't work in the long run, so eliminate them early. You cannot afford a bad choice.

  Your technical design will also include hardware choices. In some cases, your customers will choose their own hardware. If the choice is yours, choose the lowest-cost, web-based alternative on everything. Realize that it's hard enough to enter and succeed in an existing market with a cost of goods lower than your competitors'. Realize it's even harder to enter and succeed with a cost that is equal to that of your competitors, and nearly impossible to enter and succeed with a higher cost.

  A sound technical design will provide you with a long-term foundation for the business. Review and discuss the plan thoroughly. Too many products and companies are started with inadequate technical design and are doomed to early failure.

- **Development Plan.** After recording the numerous decisions you made in the previous sections of Phase II, it is time to create the development plan. This is a detailed plan of how the team will actually build the product. Here you set your standards for everything including screen displays, reports, etc. You also put down on paper the actual project plan and estimate your time to completion. This gives everyone insight into the facilities and materials needed, as well as the development personnel required to complete the project on-time.

Phase III—Prototype

During the prototype phase, you and your team will build a working version of every system designed in the design phase.

- **Why Prototype?** Building a prototype is an absolute necessity in the Zero Defects Development Program. It is the time to test all the theories and components that come together to form a product. You actually hold the product in your hand, feel the weight, evaluate the color, try out all the buttons and invariably learn a number of "better ways" to do things.

  Even more important than your perception of the product are your customers' perceptions of it. Recall, earlier in this chapter we said that the product would be successful only if it passes the user tests. The prototype is built for users, users who will now critique your efforts. Their demands are not complex. Customers simply want products that are:

  - Easy to use
  - Simple to understand
  - Interactive
  - Easy to customize or set up
  - Have fast response times
  - Work 100 percent of the time
  - Solve their problems

  By prototyping and allowing customers to provide feedback, you can make sure the product passes all these criteria before making major investments. It also gives you and your customers a chance to determine how the product compares to competitive products.

- **Functional User Interface.** The functional user interface or a limited example of it should be part of the prototype. Build at least one or two interfaces so that customers can compare and decide which one delivers the criteria above best. Choose one from a common legacy system that's familiar to the customer and one that is web-based. Take the time to make the interface experience complete by allowing the customer to interact with the device and have it respond back. In other words, when the customer presses a button, the device should actually work.

- **Demo System.** The demo system is a more advanced system prototype. The primary function of the demo system is to give a solid feel and understanding of how the device will work. In the case of a software or hardware product, the demo will show a complete flow of several different transactions. The customer should be able to evaluate the functionality based on the above criteria. Getting passable marks the first time on every customer criteria is highly unusual. To hit your objectives, plan into your project schedule time for three to four prototype efforts.

- **Customer Sign-Off.** After a great deal of work and rework, the customers will sign off. Of course the best sign-off is a signed contract to deliver and install your product upon completion. But if that doesn't happen, the next best sign-off is a candid assessment of the product and verification that it meets all the customer criteria. This sign-off should follow a thorough demonstration to the customer of the revised product.

Phase IV—System Build

With a solid prototype that has achieved customer sign-off, you are ready for the system-build stage. This is the phase when your single prototype becomes many. It's exciting and quite tempting to rush the process. Avoid the temptation, and take it one step at a time.

- **Product Development Plan.** Your development plan should include a specific list of tasks with deliverables, none of which should exceed two weeks. Development projects that are not broken down into small segments have a tendency to expand in duration and never get completed. Develop the plan, distribute it to the development team, review it and ask each team member to commit to the schedule.

  You'll want to assign a project leader who has the responsibility of making sure the project is proceeding on-time and on budget.

Too often a development project with a six-month schedule is running right on schedule when the team members give their updates 30 days before the deadline. Then mysteriously, two days before the scheduled completion date, one or more team members announce that the project is going to be 60 days late. Programmers are not at fault. It's the fault of management and the project leader. Projects with long lead times need intermediate checkpoints. Without them, the bulk of the real work tends to slide into the last 20 percent of the time frame. When that occurs you have zero chance of finishing on-time.

- **Product Development Testing.** All development team members must thoroughly test each of their segments; that is a given. How involved must these tests be? In the Zero Defects Development Program, the tests are extensive. They must test every combination of data in all possible conditions and record a pass or fail. A sophisticated programming approach to development may reduce the coding effort, but it can dramatically increase the development testing. When deadlines become short, developers must resist the temptation to short circuit the testing of individual segments or programs. More than one product has failed because the testing of segments never happened. In fact, most failed products are a result of inadequate testing.

  There is no mystery to satisfying customers; it is actually very easy. They simply expect the products they buy to work 100 percent of the time. The only way you can satisfy this customer expectation is if you test 100 percent of the options in each segment.

- **User Documentation.** This may sound backwards, but the Zero Defects Development Program requires the completion of user documentation before you complete the product. The reason is understandable when you consider that the documentation becomes a key part of the testing. It helps assure that the product does what the company says it does in the documentation.

  Customers often use documentation to install and set up the product for the first time or use it as a reference when something goes wrong. Poor documentation can make a bad customer situation worse, so make sure the documentation will calm customers rather than enflame them more. In other words, make a good first impression and be the solution provider in times of trouble. Hire a documentation specialist who knows how people use user manuals, online help and other types of technical documentation. You need an experienced professional for this important job.

- **Training Programs.** Transferring the product from development to a sales and support environment will require training for all functional areas of the company as well as for the customer. Training programs should cover the product thoroughly but also be tailored to each specific group. For example, users of a software application will need to know how to operate it so that they can increase their productivity in their daily work. Customers who are charged with installing and maintaining that software program will need to know how to set up securities, user preferences, file maintenance and more. A good training program can make a good product outstanding. Inadequate training can make a good product seem complex, ineffective and substandard.

Phase V—Transition

During the transition phase, the product migrates from the development department into other departments to and persons out of the development team's control. It's a big step in the development of any product, and it means the product must be good enough to stand on its own, without development team intervention, from this point forward.

- **Quality Assurance.** Some people think the quality assurance department is where the testing begins. Actually, it is where the testing ends. The product-testing process moves to quality assurance only after the development team has thoroughly tested all the program segments. The quality assurance department performs three important tests that determine the overall quality of the product. Those tests are a comprehensive system test, a volume test and a response-time test.

  ‣ The comprehensive system tests all segments together from the beginning of the system to the end. The quality assurance team should document this test plan so that they can use it for subsequent product releases.

  ‣ The volume test determines how many transactions per second the product can process with specific hardware configurations.

> ⬥ Response-time testing identifies a response-time goal and determines how many transactions the system will process while varying the numbers of users and still maintaining the response-time goal.

The team that performs the quality-assurance testing should be different than the persons who designed the product. Ideally, the quality-assurance team should report to the customer service department rather than product development to minimize any conflicts of interest or politics. Under no circumstances should the developers check their own work. As the product proceeds through quality assurance, pay careful attention to all errors and the programmer who created them. Look for patterns and then take corrective action when necessary.

- **Beta Testing.** Beta testing involves a live test of the product in one or more customers' offices. Select your beta sites carefully, choosing customers who are committed to really using the product during the test. A beta test is purposeless if the tester doesn't use the product to the extent necessary to test it. Closely monitor each test site and individual tester. Call them frequently and discuss the product's performance. When problems arise and testers call for advice or information, respond immediately. These early test sites will be a great source of early sales, customer testimonials and publicity.

Phase VI—General Release

Once the product is ready for production, schedule multiple builds with multiple shipments on a controlled basis. Forecast wisely and utilize as many just-in-time processes as possible. This is the final step in the conversion from a development company to a marketing and sales organization.

The Zero Defects Development Program—Services

Services come into being somewhat differently than products. There may or may not be a tangible product to build and test, but there always are a series of actions and activities to execute and evaluate. Just like the development of products, the best services are born out of customer need and evaluated by customers at every juncture.

In some cases, as your organization is developing a product it must also develop the companion service for it. Look at your core product or service as the bull's-eye in a target. Surrounding that bull's-eye are from six to 20 or more services that the customer considers to be part of the total product. Poor performance in any support area will make even a great product a mediocre or poor one in the eyes of consumers. Consider:

- **Packaging.** What does the customer receive and in what condition?
- **Installation.** How quick, easy and bug free is the un-boxing and installation?
- **Customer Inquiries.** Do you have an empowered customer service department?
- **Rework Capability.** Does the product or service need one or two additions to make it perfect?
- **Invoicing.** How clear is the invoice received by the customer?
- **Credit Memo Policies.** Unfortunately some products are returned. How quickly does the accounting department react?
- **Customer Training.** Do you have an educational system available for customers?
- **Communication Response.** Are customer calls or emails regarded as opportunities or ills that must be handled?

These are just a few of the support services needed to round out your service or product. You must have a zero-defects product or service to compete in the business arena. By itself, that's not enough; you also have to have outstanding internal support services.

The Developer Psyche

Typical developers of products and services are very proud. They are proud of their creative abilities and of their products' abilities to contribute to the greater good. They hold a great deal of passion. In a performance review, they usually will not argue their case, feeling their performance speaks for itself. Take care of the developers and compensate them fairly, because they can work anywhere. Know that they are more committed to their work than they are to the company or to you. They will seldom leave in the middle of a project; rather, they will complete their tasks and then leave. Appreciate their gifts. An experienced development team can set an example of excellence that is difficult for any other functional area to match. They will build the products that form a foundation for company strength and longevity. You will inspire them, and they will inspire you back.

An Empowered Customer Service Department

Customer service is your knowledge bank.
Use what they know to improve.
When empowered to lead a company,
These people can achieve extraordinary results.

A key ingredient for outstanding customer service is an empowered customer service department. Empowered customer service principles make the customer service department agents of change. The only way to evolve to this higher state of being is to make sure the customer service manager has a status and rank equal to any officer within the company. This legitimizes the department and makes a statement that the company is serious about customer service. If you don't give power to customer service, the entire function becomes a catch basin for all the company's problems, with little chance of ever becoming valuable to anyone—the customers or the company. Each customer service representative should have the authority to direct change within other functional areas of the company based on accumulated consumer feedback. Customer service personnel should have the power and the responsibility to point out product or process problems that undermine customer satisfaction or customer service's ability to effectively carry out its duties.

Does any company really have an excuse not to have exceptional customer service? After all, the people who work for companies are customers too. They know what it's like to receive poor service. Certainly, they themselves have been on hold for 45 minutes to solve a 30-second problem. They've talked to customer service representatives who demanded lengthy explanations only to respond that they can't actually solve the 30-second problem. They've run problems up the flag pole, explaining and re-explaining to shift leaders, managers and finally to vice presidents who ultimately say, "No problem," and expect customer elation despite the wasted hours.

What can anyone do in a situation like this? Well, if you're like the majority of Americans, you tell your friends about it. But you don't just tell one friend or two; statistics say you tell approximately ten people about a bad customer experience. Word gets around quickly, which is unfortunate. A reputation for bad customer service isn't the kind of buzz any company wants or needs.

Since all entrepreneurs are customers as well as company executives, their difficulty providing exceptional customer service can't be caused by a lack of empathy or desire. It must be a lack of knowledge, commitment and execution that holds them back. Almost every company has a customer service department, but few have effective customer service. Many companies just accept their mediocre customer service because they think this is the best they can do. They don't know how to do it any better. Until the company empowers customer service they will continue to struggle with this critical company function.

Point of Contact

The customer service representative is the most important point of contact your company will have with the customer. Interactions between customer service representatives and the customers can create long-term goodwill or be a disaster when the representative cannot solve the problem. Customer service is the direct line of communication to the customer, and you, the entrepreneur, are wise to support their efforts and applaud their ability to purify the company's products and services.

A single point of contact, meaning one person handles the entire service call, is the best plan of action for any customer service process. The best service comes from the fewest number of people interfacing with the client. Customers should not have to repeat their stories to multiple people to get their problems solved. Even when the problem demands technical help or research, the customer service representative is responsible for obtaining the technical help, performing the necessary research and reporting back to the customer. Transfer the customer and you've severely impacted the quality of service.

Some customer service departments assign representatives to specific accounts. By its very nature, this system means the representatives will not be available 100 percent of the time. Other individuals should be on hand to field the calls, record the issues and document any follow-up items. The customer service representative who owns that account is responsible for verifying with the client that everything was handled satisfactorily.

Standards of Performance

Customer service must establish standards of performance for its own department and the other functional areas in the company that must support it. In addition, any area that may work directly with the customer must have standards of performance. The standards of performance should have five items:

1. Definition of the function
2. Estimate of how long it will take
3. Completion and delivery dates
4. Explanation of cost to the customer
5. Percent on-time service delivery experienced

In association with other departments, customer service will need to identify and commit to delivering these standards of performance. The commitment must be company-wide.

Customer Expectation

Your company's standards of performance will become your customers' expectation level. Meet or exceed it, and you will have very satisfied customers. Go anywhere below it, and your customers will either be quite vocal about it, or they will quietly slip away to your competitors.

Establish the standards of performance in early conversations by reviewing it with every prospect during the sales cycle. Then review it again after the prospect becomes a customer. Of course, there are times when specific customers may require higher levels of service and attention. Often these exceptions are minor and very simple to perform. The rest may take more effort, but the effort is worth the work. Remember, the most important thing to an entrepreneur is a customer. After all, developing a new customer is far more expensive than nurturing an existing one.

Two Types of Service—Actual and Perceived

There are two types of service: actual and perceived. Actual service requirements are defined by your company's sales and marketing brochures, its contract and the other commitments it makes to the customer. How company representatives fulfill those commitments is your level of actual service. Perceived service is the customer's perception of the service the company provides. It's measured with each customer, and you can dramatically improve customer perceptions simply by increasing the quality and frequency of communications with the customer. The Internet is making this quick and inexpensive. Particularly with today's technology, it is a mistake to communicate with your customers only when problems arise. A strong communication link between the customer and the company is essential. Proper communication with customers will make poor service look better and good service look outstanding. To be successful, you need only to honor your commitments and communicate the results to the customer. Those few who honor their commitments will stand alone and become revered.

The actual service rating and the perceived service rating are not necessarily the same. It's possible to have a high actual service rating and a low perceived service rating or vice versa. Perception, because it's the customer's rating, becomes reality. This is the rating that your company must address and work continually to improve.

Quality Circles

When you empower customer service to be the ears and the voice of the customer, change is inevitable. As during the development process when customers suggested changes to product design, customer comments will suggest changes to the way people in the company work. The problem is that some individuals will be reluctant to make changes in their areas just because a customer is occasionally inconvenienced.

To eliminate the perception that customer service is telling everyone what to do and how to do it, you can establish quality circles. A quality circle consists of individuals from different departments who discuss and arrive at recommendations to solve company-wide issues. They also help identify problems that are not as obvious. The results of this process can be slow, but it does raise the cooperation level among departments—highly valuable if change is ever to occur.

Customer Service Database

The most effective customer service departments run from one centralized customer database that includes a wealth of data for everyone in the company to view at any time. The database should contain all the vital information about the customer, a chronological list of customer inquiries, customer problems and customer comments. In addition, each interaction should indicate any follow-up required plus a current file of all unresolved items and unfulfilled actions.

All staff, regardless of department, should update the central file with each customer interaction. Obviously, a web-based system with high-level security and encryption is the recommended format.

Customer Service Quality

Customer service excellence tends to drive higher levels of performance in all departments. Ironically, customer service by itself cannot improve actual service to the customer. They need cooperation from all areas, and that cooperation can be elusive. It's paramount that senior management aggressively supports customer service's efforts toward higher quality. When this support happens the voice of the customer is heard and acted upon. Real change happens, and the result is not only satisfied customers but also a growing company reputation for responsiveness and customer care.

Customer Service Development Input

The customer service department is like having a customer focus group in house at all times. They are talking to the customers daily, taking notes on the good, the bad and the ugly of every product or service and every feature of those products or services. That's valuable knowledge that companies pay large sums of money to get through customer research. Smart companies use this information to improve their product design, service requirements and documentation on an ongoing basis. The result is overall cost savings, improved products and services and fewer calls to customer service.

Customer Service Action Plan

To implement an effective customer service department, you'll need at a minimum the following:

- **Empowered Customer Service.** Make this the philosophy of the operation.
- **Customer Database.** Create detailed record of information and interactions.
- **Customer Service Training.** Cover the products, the company, phone manner.
- **Technical Support Liaison.** Designate a specific person and that person's availability.
- **Call-back Guidelines.** Address every unresolved issue with the client on a regular, predetermined basis.
- **Response Guidelines for Support Areas.** Define these rules for each area.
- **Communication Protocols.** Establish procedures for phone, email and the Web.

The Elevation of Customer Service

Many companies treat customer service as a glorified complaint department or as a suggestion box with no slot. That's very unenlightened thinking. There's gold in the customer service team when they are properly empowered. A good customer service team with the appropriate authority can change your overall customer satisfaction level from unsatisfactory to outstanding within three to six months. When that happens, your growth rate and your income will both increase. The reasons are simple. Customers become more satisfied, so they buy more products and recommend your products to others. The sales cycle shortens because customers and prospects are already sold on your company, and attrition rates decrease because as your company gets stronger, the competition looks weaker. Empower customer service, support them 100 percent, stand back and get ready to grow. Remember, growth is not a goal; it is a reward for performance.

An Employee-Based Strategic Planning System

And where do we go from here?
Who has the right to point the way?
Don't individuals have a voice?
Everyone wants to find success.

Strategic Planning. If the sound of those two words echoes ominously in your brain like a promo for your late-night shock theater, then you've probably been through the agony of a typical strategic planning process. You know the drill. The CFO piles tons of extra work on your already overloaded schedule and expects you to not only do your regular job, but also come up with a realistic budget for the coming year. Never mind that you've never actually seen this year's budget in full; that isn't important. Your challenge is to shape your own destiny or nail your own coffin with the touch of a few keystrokes on an Excel spreadsheet. Of course three months later, you're relieved to know that the terribly unrealistic strategic plan you developed is safely on top of the president's file cabinet gathering dust and just about entirely hidden by a pile of trade journals that have yet to be read. Whew! That was a close one.

Well, before you skip this chapter altogether, vowing never to take on a strategic planning project, know this: Strategic planning does not have to be painful. Strategic planning does not have to be complex. Strategic planning does not have to be a waste of time. In fact, strategic planning can be relatively easy, insightful and incredibly valuable to your company provided you keep it simple and aim for quality information that is actionable, not a quantity of information that overwhelms.

Success-driven entrepreneurs demand an Employee-Based Strategic

Planning System that captures 100 percent of their employees' creativity and engages everyone in the planning process. A creatively and thoughtfully developed strategic plan creates a blueprint for successful growth, and it gives the contributing employees a sense of involvement with the company. The plan itself becomes the vision, the direction and a useful symbol to guide the success for the company and everyone involved.

If you've hired correctly, you'll find creativity in all levels of your company. The goal of Employee-Based Strategic Planning is to extract that creativity from employees for the good of the company and the good of their own careers.

Many entrepreneurs are astonished the first time they are confronted with the creative ideas generated by lower-level employees. The surprise extends further once the entrepreneur and executive team discover that employees who are asked their opinions about how things should work develop a stronger bond with the company. Loyalty increases and a sense of personal ownership takes effect. The result is a noticeable, measurable boost in productivity and performance.

In fact, as a new business leader, it is in your best interest to become one with the strategic planning process described in this chapter. Even if you don't feel you need it now, you will need it later. All entrepreneurs must challenge their own competency at every level of their company's growth. Do you and your staff possess the intelligence, mental toughness and skill set to take the company to the next level of growth? Can you and your key leaders execute your growth by yourselves? Perhaps in the short run, but somewhere, between $2 million and $20 million in annual revenue, the answer becomes a definite no!

Achieving real growth requires participation from all employees. An individual cannot grow a company without the help of management and employees. If you recognize that it is impossible to achieve success alone, congratulations! You have figured out the first step to being successful.

There isn't a single executive alive who has not gone through the same self-assessment process. Of course, there's a little ego. You have the know-how, the experience and the creativity to make the company great. There may even be a little scrimping. After all, why should you pay for something you can do yourself? There may even be a bit of wishful thinking. Wouldn't it be great to never have to manage people ever again? Those entrepreneurs who fail to make the leap from me to us, from one to many, from I to you and from an individual autocrat to a mass of involvement will not realize their company's true potential.

Traditional Planning

Traditionally, most small businesses focus on a two- or three-year time horizon for their strategic plans. The plan construction takes place in the accounting department, and capital asset requests drive the decision making. Accountants match requested asset purchases with projected available cash and management priorities, then merge them until the resulting report outlines a probable spending pattern for the next two or three years.

This outline of probable spending, along with sales forecasts for available products, takes the form of a budget for the next 12 months and a "strategic plan" for the subsequent year or two. This work of art is a prime candidate for the top of the president's file cabinet where it will be neatly tucked within a row of other presentations from years past. It's an exercise in futility and an enormous waste of time.

By contrast, the Employee-Based Strategic Plan involves all employees, solicits input from each and every one, and identifies company strengths, weaknesses, threats and opportunities. By involving all employees, the strategic plan becomes their own, not just the plan of the entrepreneur or the executive staff. Employees involved in strategic planning will develop a greater sense of company pride, enthusiasm in their work, and a great deal more energy and effort in all they do. Productivity skyrockets dramatically.

The Preplanning Booklet

The preplanning booklet is your starting point for the Employee-Based Strategic Plan. This booklet includes vital information regarding the company's direction and the planning process itself. It is critical if you hope to receive quality input from employees. Helping employees see the big picture process and understand what is expected of them will also make the system more efficient. Specifically, the preplanning booklet should include:

▶ Outline of planning process (timing, steps, responsibilities)

▶ Corporate objectives

- Baseline planning
- Definition of strengths, weaknesses, threats and opportunities
- Specific input forms
- Instructions for completion of input forms

Outline of Planning Process (Timing, Steps, Responsibility)

Too often, companies try to do everything in October or November of the current year in an effort to be ready on January 1 with the new plan. It doesn't take long before the companies realize this is an impossible task and get disenchanted with whole strategic planning process. The following table will guide you and your organization with planning tasks throughout the year. It will help make the process manageable and signal to all employees that you are empathetic to their daily work pressures. With this timetable, you are not asking the impossible.

TIME	PROJECT	LEAD RESPONSIBILITY
Last quarter of current year	Develop next year's MBOs (management by objectives)	Entrepreneur, senior management
	Create financial plan	CFO, senior management
First quarter of current year	Baseline planning and gap analysis	Entrepreneur, CFO
	Develop preplanning workbook	CFO
Second quarter of current year	Distribute preplanning workbook	CFO
	Training sessions for all managers and employees	CFO
	Fill out input forms	All managers and employees
Third quarter of current year	Department meetings for input roll-ups	Department meetings with all employees
	Functional area roll-ups	Managers
	Selection of strengths, weaknesses, opportunities, threats for next year	Entrepreneur, senior management
	Growth objectives for next three years	Entrepreneur, CFO
Fourth quarter of current year	Same as last quarter of current year above	

1. **Corporate Objectives.** From the management by objectives system, corporate objectives are nothing more than a roll-up listing all managers' goals. The company uses these objectives as input for the current year's financial plan and budget.

2. **Baseline Planning and Gap Analysis.** This evaluation of your company's revenue potential helps you determine your expected sales versus your desired sales for the coming year. The first step is to determine next year's sales projection. To do this, look at price increases, inflationary price adjustments, product additions or deletions, growth in your customer base and any other forces that could affect next year's sales. Without any major changes, what is the projected sales revenue for the next three years? What is the growth rate percentage? What should it be? Are you profitable? If you are not profitable, address this issue first because profitability opens doors to sources of capital that you'll need for growth. If you are profitable, how much are you willing to spend to facilitate growth?

    Your desired growth rate is a judgment decision. When your company is small, a 40 to 50 percent increase over the previous year is possible. When the company is larger, 15 percent to 30 percent may be more realistic. You should attempt to grow at a faster rate than the market you serve, which means you must continually increase your market share.

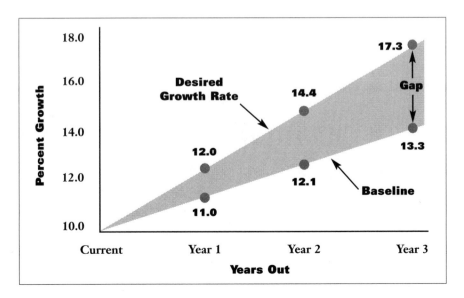

To achieve your desired sales goals you must determine how to fill in the gap. In most cases, this is accomplished though entry into new geographical areas, increased marketing and sales activities, new products and services introductions and acquisitions. Ask your employees how to fill in the gap. You will be surprised by what they tell you.

3. **Definition of Strengths, Weaknesses, Threats, Opportunities.** This section is the heart and soul of the strategic plan. By determining your company's strengths, weaknesses, threats and opportunities, you get a real-life view of where your company stands and what it needs to do to grow. Once you have the information, it is meaningless unless you act on it. Here are some guidelines:

   - *Strengths.* Ask your employees what they think the company does well The answers yield your company's strengths. Once armed with this information, build on it, emphasize your strengths in your marketing and sales materials and use them to create pride and enthusiasm within the company.

   - *Weaknesses.* Ask your employees what they feel needs to be improved within the company. These are your weaknesses. Eliminate them. Weaknesses will be discovered in many areas, most of which affect customers or employees. Frequently, they will revolve around communication. You can eliminate most of them with minimal time and effort. This should be a top priority.

   - *Threats.* Seek to discover major factors, such as government regulations or laws, new competitors, loss of key employees or catastrophic events that could cripple the business. Know your threats and set up contingency plans.

   - *Opportunities.* Consider new business opportunities for products or services and new market opportunities. This is how you fill the gap between your baseline and your desired growth rate.

4. **Specific Input Forms.** Two input forms will yield a wealth of information, and they are very much alike. The first form solicits input for an employee's own department. The other is for the company as a whole. Ask all employees to complete both forms. Department personnel know the issues within their own areas. This is their chance to speak up about them without any backlash or repercussions. The second form gives all employees the chance

to critique the rest of the company as well. The two input forms that follow help you gather constructive, focused information.

After the employees complete these forms, the manager collects the information and summarizes the group's input in a departmental meeting. The manager then forwards the information to the next level of authority within the company, where all information is summarized into one report that lists all the comments and suggestions and includes a count for the number of times employees mentioned each entry. Once senior management reviews the final report, they incorporate key items from the summary into next year's management by objectives or quality plans. Selection of actionable items happens on a priority basis, with items not on the priority list being held for the second or third year. Every item is not a good idea, but you must consider every item and keep all employees informed about the ones you have selected for action.

Critique Form for Your Area

SWOT Analysis

Name

Department

Date

Objective Class
1. Marketing
2. Innovation
3. Personnel Resources
4. Financial Resources
5. Physical Resources
6. Productivity
7. Social Responsibility
8. Financial Responsibility

Item	Class
Strengths	
1	
2	
3	
4	
5	
Weaknesses	
1	
2	
3	
4	
5	
Threats	
1	
2	
3	
4	
5	
Opportunities	
1	
2	
3	
4	
5	

Critique For the Rest of Your Company

SWOT Analysis			

Objective Class
1. Marketing
2. Innovation
3. Personnel Resources
4. Financial Resources
5. Physical Resources
6. Productivity
7. Social Responsibility
8. Financial Responsibility

Name _____

Department _____

Date _____

Item	Dept.	Class
Strengths		
1		
2		
3		
4		
5		
Weaknesses		
1		
2		
3		
4		
5		
Threats		
1		
2		
3		
4		
5		
Opportunities		
1		
2		
3		
4		
5		

Importance of Follow Through

Once started by the entrepreneur, the entire process does not automatically run to completion; it is extra work that requires thought and energy. Some groups or departments do not participate. A few managers become bottlenecks, and some employees feel threatened. As the entrepreneur and the leader, you need to stay on top of the process by staying on top of the senior management team. They must make sure everyone participates. Look for people who are not participating and uncover the reasons for non-participation. Often the reasons reveal weaknesses in your organization. Identify them and make the necessary changes.

Input Characteristics

The input you receive from your employees differs based on their level of responsibility within your company. Typically, the following patterns hold true:

- **Senior Management.** Their issues tend to be "global" in nature and more focused on bigger issues, primarily marketing, sales and product concerns. Their subjects track consistently with the entrepreneur, but their views will be much different.

- **Managers and Supervisors.** Their primary issues revolve around communications—with customers, employees and the community. To be effective, you must keep managers and supervisors informed of changes in direction, objectives, product, pricing, promotion, etc. They run the company, and your productivity levels are dependent on their efforts. Through outstanding internal communications, you gain efficiencies and full employee cooperation.

- **Employees.** Employees tend to provide input in two primary areas: quality and human resource issues:

  - *Quality.* When quality is poor, frequently the problem's cause is not obvious, except to employees. Once they understand that there are no bad ideas and no recrimination they quickly point out the problems and the causes in an effort to make their own lives easier.

  - *Human resource issues.* Employees always identify items relating to pay, fringe benefits, favoritism and lack of advancement. Particularly if problems exist, these issues will rise to the surface. They are easily corrected, especially where pay is involved.

Output Objectives

As you can see, this strategic planning process is not complex. Rather, it is effective at discovering what's important to the growth of your company. In addition, through this process you should gain the following:

- Commitment of employees to the company's direction
- Recognition of the company's strengths
- Fifteen to 20 weaknesses to correct (or as many as can be addressed)

▶ Identification of potential threats

▶ Several new business opportunities

▶ Numerous items to add to the management-by-objectives system

▶ Numerous items to add to the quality plan

And last, but perhaps most important...

▶ A major step in converting the entrepreneurial company from an "I" to a "We."

Customer-Oriented Quality Control

14

**Quality is not an end point.
Quality is a journey.
We can't be perfect;
Our goal is improvement.**

Customer-Oriented Quality Control improves customer satisfaction, which is a major factor in a company's profitability, health and longevity. Satisfied customers buy more of what you're selling, buy more often, tell their friends and in general become the basis for your business. In company terms, quality is a people issue not a product or service one. What stands between your quality control policies and procedures and delivering a high- quality product or service is people. People make it happen or they don't. The sooner your employees accept that the number one determinant of long-term growth and profitability is quality, the sooner your company will be delivering quality to your customers. And it's in everyone's best interest, including your employees'.

Quality is a word spoken too often. Every company claims that their product or service is of great quality, and all their clichéd sales lines ring out loud and clear in our collective brain. They come at us so frequently that we are numb to what the words really mean. In fact, we barely hear the claims of quality anymore because they are so redundant and routine. Are they really believable? For companies that have built their reputations on quality, we may believe their claims and buy their products or services with confidence. However, for companies that are unknown and claim to deliver quality, seeing is believing. Young companies must repeatedly go above and beyond to demonstrate quality and to win the loyalty of new customers. Words alone will not deliver.

Well, that's a shame, because talking about quality is a lot easier than actually delivering quality. Demonstrating it daily presents challenges that a young company can't mask with a catchy marketing slogan and a slick ad. Feeling quality is what it's all about, and quality has to be managed company-wide to be felt by even just one consumer.

Expectations of Quality

Today's customers do not accept poor quality. Why should they when alternatives to your company and your products and services are everywhere? Today you need your customers more than your customers need you. While every customer has his or her own definition of quality, there are certain things that almost all customers expect when they do business with a company. Customers expect to receive on time and in perfect condition items they have ordered. Customers expect to be billed promptly and correctly. Customers expect rapid access to customer service and prompt follow-up to questions and service issues. Customers expect courteous service. They expect an empathetic ear when problems arise. They expect personal care and openness to special cases. They expect employees who are empowered to solve customers' problems. More and more, they expect round-the-clock availability. And they expect products to last and services to fulfill their needs. In short, customers expect it all!

Poor Quality Costs

Some companies are too busy to do things right the first time, but when a customer complains, they manage to find time to do them over again. What a waste of energy and opportunity! Errors in process, product or service routinely consume several times the effort and cost your company more than double the money of doing things right the first time. Even worse, they do nothing to build your reputation. Quality isn't a cost, it's an insurance policy for survival, and your level of quality is a strong predictor of how long you will remain in business. In the short term, poor quality will cost you a few sales and a few customers. Unless corrected, poor quality will, over time, damage your reputation and create negative customer perceptions you'll find challenging to change. In the long term, poor quality can cost you the dearest price of all, the failure of your company.

A Company-Wide Effort

How do you create quality within your company? Involve everyone in your organization and back the quality initiatives with all your strength and power. As the entrepreneur, you hold the key to the company's passion. You must preach quality daily. You are its champion, because with every product or service you deliver, with every letter or contract that goes out the door, your name and your pride goes with it. Preaching quality isn't enough; you need to create a foundation for a simple, results-oriented quality management system. Your management team holds the key to the success of your system. If they don't buy in, the quality initiatives will make it out the door of your office, but no farther.

Quality doesn't come from an individual, a department or a group of inspectors. It comes from any employee in your company who is consistently monitoring predefined customer satisfaction indicators such as on-time delivery, timely call-backs, etc. Each employee monitors the indicators and, more importantly, possesses the power to do what it takes to improve performance. With all employees involved, minor errors become visible and are corrected.

Quality must address major corporate functions as well, such as the level of customer involvement in new product development, customer attrition, employee turnover, corporate cash flow planning and any other issues that impact corporate viability. Every company faces unforeseen problems, but if employees effectively handle the routine, smaller issues and monitor the big issues, then when the unexpected does occur you can confront it without being overwhelmed. It takes an entire company to deliver quality. It takes the entrepreneur to lead the charge.

The Quality Goals

Quality is about improvement. There is no end to the quest for quality. It is a journey not a destination. The best quality goals stress improvement. Improved performance compared to yesterday, to last week, to last month, to last quarter and to last year. The goal is not to make or sell more of anything. The goal is to do more things correctly the first time. This by itself will increase productivity, just by working smarter.

Relate your quality goals to customer satisfaction. It is the customers' perceptions of the company that count. Serve them and you will serve yourself. Customers' perceptions of service may vary dramatically with your actual level of service. Some perceive your level of service to be better than it actually is, others may perceive it to be

lower, so take this into account. Your service is only as good as the customers perceive it to be. Solve your problems and build perceptions or
lose customers.

The Quality System

As mentioned earlier in this chapter, quality control is a function of
managing people more than policies. Before you can instruct people,
you need a system that provides direction and a course of action. The
system is simple. Each department or function selects four to seven
items within their immediate control that affect customer satisfaction.
Then they begin. Not next week, not next month when the new computer system arrives, but today. Right now, just begin. They begin by
recording the number of transactions performed and tally the number
that are performed correctly and incorrectly. On at least a weekly basis,
analyze the number that are incorrect and determine a cause. Look for
the sources of problems, and ask yourself what you can change to move
the number to zero. During the following week, each manager must do
what is necessary to bring that number to zero.

That's the basic system. It is a very straightforward, common sense
system that gets results without a great deal of extra work. All you need
is paper and a pencil. The difficulties arise from the people. Unless
everyone is committed to the process, the challenges can be overwhelming.

The People Issues

People's attitudes and behaviors can make implementing quality-control systems challenging. They require company-wide teamwork, and
the pressure's on. Often failure on the part of any of the team members
impacts the customer and the company's bottom line directly.

Customer service departments are impacted both positively and
negatively by quality-control initiatives. They can easily feel that all the
company's problems show up on their desks. It seems that they are sentenced to handling all the difficult customer situations. Not so! A good
customer service manager or any other manager will demand that other
departments embrace the program and sign on in earnest to the quality initiatives. The more people are involved in the quality programs,
the more peer pressure kicks in to force non-conformists to get on
board. For example, there's no reason why customer service should take
the blame and the black mark on its quality record for a promised deliv-

ery date that shipping approved then missed. Problems become apparent and then get resolved but not without conflict.

In fact, this overlap of responsibility will create tremendous friction during the first few months of implementing a quality program. A management team that works well together will work through the issues. The top performers will create so much stress for the laggards that poor performers will either conform or leave.

When employees who think other managers are becoming too demanding confront you or your senior officers, listen but do not usurp the authority of your managers who are working through the issues. Rather, support them 100 percent.

Baseline

With the system in place and ready to go, there are still the questions of what to measure and how to judge the level of excellence. Answer those questions by determining your baselines or starting points from which you begin to measure your quality progress. If your company does not have any basis from which to compare its progress, don't worry about it. Start right now and establish your baselines. After just 30 days, you'll have your first month's numbers in, and your comparisons can begin. Don't let idealists in the company convince you that a year's worth of data is needed to make valid comparisons. It's not true. Just start now!

The Measurements

Each functional area, department or individual-operating entity selects their own four to seven key customer satisfaction indicators to serve as points of measurement for quality progress. These are measured on a regular basis and progress is monitored. The subsequent sections identify several examples in each area to get you started developing your own measurement indicators:

Entrepreneurs and Senior Management

- What percent of personnel were involved in quality control?
- What percent of personnel were involved in strategic planning?
- What percent of employees have documented objectives and goals?
- What percent of employees have received at least 14 days of in-house or seminar training

▶ What percent of employees attended weekly meetings or received weekly emails regarding units' performance?

Marketing

▶ How many qualified leads were generated?

▶ What percent of major products had customer focus groups or significant customer input?

▶ What percent of items scheduled for completion or action were actually completed?

▶ Is the current marketing campaign consistent in message and theme? Either yes or no.

▶ What is the total cost of the marketing department divided by the number of qualified leads? (cost per lead)

Sales

▶ Were sales equal to or in excess of 85 percent of goal for the period? (list percentage)

▶ Were year-to-date sales equal to or in excess of 100 percent of goal? (list percentage)

▶ What percent of sales were at standard pricing and terms?

▶ What percent of leads were followed-up within seven days?

▶ What was the average closing cycle, from lead to close?

Operations or Manufacturing

▶ What percent of schedules were achieved on-time?

▶ What percent of scheduled completions were logged in the time period?

▶ What was the percent of up-time for major units or lines?

▶ What percent of re-work or re-run was necessary?

▶ For computer-related functions, what were the average interactive response times?

Customer Service

▶ What percent of problems were handled on the initial email or phone call?

▶ What percent call-back commitments were met on time?

▶ What percent of emails were answered within ten minutes?

▶ What percent of special projects were delivered on-time?

▶ For 24 x 7 service, what percent of the time were phones actually staffed?

Development

▶ What percent of projects were completed on time?

▶ What percent of new products were released without major defects?

▶ What percent of new product releases were fully tested?

▶ What percent of product releases attained their performance objectives?

▶ What percent of product releases were thoroughly system-tested to determine compatibility with other internal or external products?

Accounting

▶ What percent of invoices went out on-time and 100 percent correct?

▶ What was the percent of credit memos against invoices?

▶ What was the average turnaround time of sales contracts? (should be less than 24 hours)

▶ What percent of payroll checks are delivered on-time?

These lists provide a good start, but you will develop more meaningful lists for your company as you work through your quality system during the first year. This is an evolutionary process.

As you ask the questions, assign percentages that indicate your level of accomplishment for the current year, the baseline value and the variance between the two. You start from where you are and continue to build your system. The current period becomes the baseline for the next reporting cycle.

Quality Awards and Incentives

Offering employees and departments awards and incentives for quality initiatives is a great way to keep the programs top of mind and drive home the importance of quality to the company. Most companies have awards or clubs for sales people, then ignore everyone else. Sales people are important but not at the exclusion of the rest of the company.

Put a quality award program in place and give away trips, gifts, plaques, etc., for quality excellence. Honor the top 25 percent of performers from each department or team. Publish their results in a company newsletter, email or memo. Give them a platform to tell their stories of success. Recognize an annual top-quality winner as well as second- and third-place finishers. Through programs such as these, you will keep employees thinking about quality and achieve results you never imagined possible.

You may have heard of the Malcolm Baldrige Award for quality. It is a very prestigious annual award given for quality performance by companies. Don't waste your time trying to win this in your first year, but get copies of all application materials and read them thoroughly. This process will give you an appreciation and understanding of what the nation's most progressive organizations are doing to remain competitive with quality. After you have a quality system in place for three or four years, then maybe you'll be qualified to compete for the Baldrige Award. In the meantime, study the materials and apply what makes sense for your organization. Before you jump in with both feet, however, evaluate if the cost of competing for the award is worth more to the company than adding two sales people. Quality control doesn't have to be complex and costly; it just has to deliver results.

When it comes to quality, keep it simple. You are trying to keep track of processes and procedures that affect customers. Keep improving your performance quarter by quarter and year by year. Quality is not a cost, it is not a burden, it is not difficult. Quality is a blessing, a gift! A true formula for success: Quality goes up, then customer satisfaction goes up. When customer satisfaction goes up, customers buy more and return less. You work smarter so costs go down. The result is increased profitability and success. What could be better?

Constantly Improving Operations Performance

Today is the first day to pursue perfection.
Our efforts represent us to the world.
We work with machines and systems,
But our performance completes the process.

Professional and amateur athletes know what it takes to endure the extreme physical demands of their sports. Whether it be running, swimming, boxing, gymnastics, football or basketball, their bodies all rely on the heart to fuel the muscles they need to perform. In fact, the heart fuels every cell in the body and is responsible not just for extreme performance but everyday activities like walking, breathing, seeing, thinking, and everything else that we do. The heart is the center, and a healthy cardiovascular system is a must for quality and quantity of life. Everyday we see people walking, running and stair mastering their ways to heart health and strengthening this operations center of the human body. It's a continual effort in conditioning and reconditioning with the result being an efficient, highly productive organ that feeds an active, changing body.

Like the human heart, your operations center is the heart of your business. Just as your heart supplies blood to every muscle, bone and organ in your body, your operations center supplies vital goods and services to customers, employees, perhaps even outside clients who have contracted with you for service. Information systems centers, manufacturing plants, call centers, flight operation centers, research repositories and distribution centers are all examples of operations centers. They provide the central point and the pathway to bring life and energy to every endeavor your company tackles. Within a company, when the operations center is heart healthy, there's a good chance the company is too.

Just like an athlete, a company must continually develop its own heart center. Daily workouts are a requirement to stay fit and on top of the game. And that's probably the biggest difference between being part of operations and being part of an operations center that is continually improving its level of performance. There is no sitting still, only continual improvements that increase the performance of the entire company and give it the competitive edge. In an operations center, improvements in performance include productivity improvements, cost reductions, uptime improvements, technology enhancements, lower scrap costs, higher production rates, plus a constant search for improving the level of service to your customers. In the end, it is those you serve through the operations center—your customers, fellow employees or outside clients—who are the final judges of your performance.

Any operations center is only as good as its people and the tools they use. One without the other or one operating at a higher capacity than the other is like a heart with a faulty valve. The heart is pumping blood, certainly, and the body is living but nowhere near its potential. All valves must be pumping at full capacity to excel. For an operations center that means you need the right people, the right technology and a constantly improving operations performance to make the body that is the company work.

Staffing

The person you select to run your operations center needs one thing above all else: Experience. Assuming you like this person and that he or she possesses the maturity to handle the job, it really comes down to experience. This function of your company is too important to turn over to even the most eager Master's degree graduate fresh out of school. While inexperienced people may have the education and the technical expertise, they most often lack the interpersonal skills necessary for this position. Operations vice presidents do not hibernate in front of a computer or in a manufacturing facility. They are in the middle of everything day in and day out with all eyes focusing on them. Everyone looks to them for productivity, making this position very high profile and very high pressure.

For example, in one entrepreneurial company, the vice president of operations was responsible for not only ensuring that their products were manufactured and out the door, he was responsible for ensuring long lead-time parts were available and in stock, that staffing was on hand for assembly and that all product orders actually shipped prior to the quarter close so the company could make its numbers. On the other side, he was responsible for keeping capital expenses and costs down by not having too many parts on hand, managing part obsolescence and keeping staffing costs to a minimum. The balancing act was almost ridiculous. But ridiculous or not, these were and are just some of the realities of the operations vice president. It takes a special person with an attention to detail, a solid view of the big picture, excellent managerial skills and the ability to work well with people. This is a person who gets things done with finesse and ease.

Technology Choices

Make great technology choices and your company has the potential to soar. Make poor ones and your company will be at a severe competitive disadvantage. Technology is the great differentiator in business, because it can produce great efficiencies in operations or great inefficiencies. If your whole industry is inefficient, perhaps it seems your own inefficiency doesn't matter. But chances are there are technology-savvy players in your industry or they will soon emerge. The best advice is let that be you!

There are some important considerations when it comes to selecting and monitoring the performance of the technology that runs your company. These are a some of the biggest ones you'll encounter:

Operating System Selection

First, select one well-proven operating system and strive to make it the standard throughout the company. Most companies can operate in a Windows environment with great efficiency. Graphic design, printing and any of the graphic arts function better on Mac-based systems. Very data-intensive companies, such as those involved in research, need the power of Unix systems. Other companies that process continual transactions, such as insurers and lenders, need mainframe systems. Sometimes achieving an operating-system standard is not possible, but recognize in most companies that it is. This is not the time to prove to others how adept you and your organization are at integrating and managing very complicated networks.

Application Software Selection

Application software, such as word processing, databases, etc., are the next considerations. There are numerous choices, and the important note here is to fully analyze your needs before you select your applications. An experienced operations vice president will know to ask all employees not just what applications they need, but also what work they do on a regular basis. This tactic provides insight not only regarding application preferences, but also underlying technology needs about which they may not even be aware. With this information, your operations team will be equipped to look for economies and efficiencies company-wide versus departmental island by departmental island.

Technology Cost Versus Value

Keep in mind that system and application software will be much less expensive for PC and MAC file servers than for Unix or mainframe servers. Since having a lower-cost base in any industry is a huge competitive advantage, before you choose the more expensive operating system option, you'll want to weigh the drawbacks of having higher operations costs with the efficiencies those systems can potentially deliver.

Application Scope

How far reaching should your data processing applications be within your company? Logic says that today, you should gear your information systems towards eventually handling every application, even specialized ones. That leads to the boxed versus built dilemma. Should you fit your needs into off-the-shelf software or build your own custom applications that meet your every need? We'll cover that later in this chapter.

If you are in the software or services business and make a living out of helping other companies solve their own technology challenges, consider writing only the key applications within your area of specialty and become an authorized distributor for the necessary support applications. This will increase your efficiency and limit the non-revenue-generating demands on your customer service department.

Prioritizing Applications

When building a company there are so many needs, particularly in the areas of technology, and given limited resources of time and money, it is difficult to know what to focus on first. Experience shows that you invest in the accounting application first and your customer/marketing databases second. Think about it. Your accounting systems help you make sure that you are managing your payroll, tax deposits, accounts receivable, accounts payable, cash flow and overall financial health of the company. This is the system that keeps employees happy and accountable. It should come first.

Your customer and marketing databases are the next most important systems. To be a successful company, implement good business habits early. Begin with the very first customer and enter all customer data into your database. This database will rapidly become an extremely valuable asset to your company and will be the source of your revenue now and in the future.

Next, look at the applications that will impact most people's productivity and invest in those. Office suites that include word processing and spreadsheets are the most likely candidates. In every instance, try to stay with simple packages that you can install quickly and easily. The goal with information systems is to create a measurable competitive advantage. If you do not, someone else will.

Building Versus Buying Software

It is always a better idea to buy packaged applications because they install quicker and get you and your company productive faster. They also tend to require less maintenance. Custom-built software presents a host of problems, not the least of which can include escalating costs, missed deadlines, application bugs, difficulty of use, obsolescence and numerous others. You wouldn't be the first company to pay dearly for custom application software that was anything but effective, and that's assuming the software was completed at all.

Only an applications systems builder should build software. Even then, he or she should build only the core requirements. Part-time builders who have other duties within your organization are seldom effective at both jobs. When you can find packages that ten or more users within your industry are using effectively, the package is probably free of major bugs. Only buy what you have thoroughly tested and validate that it actually performs as represented. You'll find less than 50 percent will pass your tests.

Monitoring Up-Time

Ninety-eight percent may earn you an A in college, but in the information systems realm it scores an F. Current technology combined with good management is easily capable of 99.99 percent up-time, during both prime-time and off hours. Strive for perfection and eliminate a great deal of aggravation—company employees' and your own.

Monitoring Response Time

Technology should not interrupt the flow of productivity. Computer systems that force workers to wait five to ten seconds for a response to commands are unacceptable. They inhibit and frustrate workers. Subsecond response time is attainable in a properly functioning information system. Occasionally, data searches may take more time, but if you find that users request frequent searches, you'll need to upgrade your system with additional indices.

Application Completeness

Unless your system performance—up-time and response time—is satisfactory, the completeness of the under-performing applications isn't important. Your employees won't use them anyway, so it doesn't really matter what that application contains or what it is missing.

Assuming your operations team is meeting the performance standards, they will need to constantly monitor each application for effectiveness and make any necessary changes to enhance productivity. For example, your first payroll system may be great for ten or 20 employees but a disaster for 200. The goal is to stay ahead of the company's growth curve and build more capacity than currently needed into every system.

Internet Power

Mobility and working remotely are fundamental to modern business. Keep people productive while away from the office by ensuring right from the start that all applications are web based. This will give employees instant and easy access to the systems they use daily whether they are in an airport, at home or in a hotel. Installing systems that are not web based is like entering the ring with one hand tied behind your back.

Keeping Up with Technology

Keep up with all software releases once they have become accepted. You don't have time to become a test site for the software, but after a significant number of your vendor's customers have upgraded, you should, too. This is not to say that you are a company that follows. On the contrary, there are times when you will lead, as discussed in the next section.

Additionally, and on a regular basis, renew your hardware platforms, PCs and network configurations. Sometimes it's those minor upgrades, such as adding extra RAM, upgrading a processor or investing in a new file server, that can result in major performance improvements system-wide.

Moving to New Technology

This is the area where you can really gain the competitive advantage, but migrate to new technology with caution. Test everything thoroughly off-line, and convert only when you are positive you can integrate the system without any drop in up-time or response time. You will need to make technology changes to stay competitive and to occasionally leapfrog everyone. You'll never have more fun than when your technology gives you an obvious edge over your competitors.

Operations Training

Continual training is important in any company and in every department, but in operations it is particularly so. Errors can happen, but when they happen in operations, they can be far reaching. Establishing procedures and training for all operations employees and following them to the letter is critical. Because operations is constantly improving systems, they'll need regular training programs to make sure everyone is aware of and implementing the latest improvements. Although it happens frequently, it is a mistake to allow operations to grow careless with training. The results can be disastrous, including everything from product defects to productivity losses to malpractice and more. If operations is the heart of your company, make sure the operations team is in training continually.

Operations Management

Managing the operations center is one of the most important and challenging positions in the company. As stated earlier, it takes a special person with experience and strong interpersonal skills. Decisions made in operations impact the entire company in most cases. To ensure that everyone is making the best decisions and carrying them out with excellence, here are a few areas to keep in mind:

Operations Appearance

If the operations area looks like a mess, it probably is a mess. Even if it is not in a state of chaos, appearances do matter because perception is reality. Any effective operations center requires organization and discipline. A neatly organized and orderly workplace is an indicator of those qualities. Furthermore, the inevitable growth of your company is impossible with a disorderly, disorganized operations center. Insist on organization and discipline in this area, and evaluate workers on this criteria if necessary.

Promote from Within

As your operations center grows, whenever possible, promote from within. Posting all jobs will alert you to people who want to move up within the organization and give proven performers a motivating career path. Of course, it causes operations managers to lose some of their departmental workhorses, people who get things done, but you'll lose these people anyway if you stifle the racehorse within.

Maintain Control

The operations center should know exactly which jobs or processes the operations team is handling at any given time. Control comes when the operations vice president is able to verify that the appropriate actions took place on any given day, understand the reasons why they did not and be empowered to make the necessary changes to ensure they do in the future. Control means knowing how many jobs were scheduled and how many were actually completed.

Manage Others' Assets

Your operations center employees are in custodial jobs. You trust them to manage and take care of the company's assets. Successful operations center people are either owner advocates or company advocates. Everything they do has to be in the best interest of the owner or the company. They may be using the assets in the normal course of business, but they still belong to the owner or the company. You'll want to make this responsibility very clear and take action for any abuses.

Lease Versus Purchase

You've read this throughout this book, but particularly in a constantly improving operations center, lease rather than purchase. In a new business, cash is always precious so leasing makes the best sense. Of course, lease all assets that become obsolete quickly, such as computer equipment. Purchase, when bank financing is available, only the assets you'll keep long term and that have minimal obsolescence. A new business in a high-growth environment should probably lease almost everything, because you will typically outgrow those assets within five years.

It's the heart that nourishes the body. Your operations center is beating 24 hours a day, seven days a week in most cases. An operations center that is fit and operating at peak performance is foundational to a company that is a leader in its industry. When every operational issue is a hurdle, rife with indecision and lack of knowledge, then the entire company suffers. Choose the right leader, equip him or her with the right tools, train everyone continually and use good business judgment when making decisions. Instill the philosophy of Constantly Improving Operations Performance. The result will be good for the operations center and the company.

Selling Your Dream

Selling Your Dream Three Times

Every business eventually will change ownership.
After yours is sold, what will you do?
Retire, start another business, or be a mentor?
Will you use your years of experience?

It all started with a dream, a wild idea that people were quick to say would never work. Now it is a dream fulfilled with people saying "I knew you when." At some point the business you and your team have built through the hard work and dedication described in this book will grow to have significant value. People will want to share in the success by owning a piece of the company themselves, perhaps the same people who dismissed your idea years before. Try not to laugh out loud when they say they knew the idea would be a success all along!

When first-time entrepreneurs think about selling their companies, they think about selling it once. You can sell it once, but you can also sell it multiple times. If you think about selling your business at least three times, chances are that one of those transactions will be a big hit financially, rewarding you, your team and all shareholders.

The First Sale

Once your company has achieved enough size (which will vary by industry), adequate profitability and can demonstrate upwards of 20 percent revenue and income-before-tax growth, you are a candidate for an initial public offering (IPO). Also called "taking your company public," this for many entrepreneurs is considered the Holy Grail of entrepreneurship—and for just reason. This is the first chance to hit it big.

Know from the start, though that on the day you go public, existing stockholders like yourself and other early investors cannot sell the new public shares you've earned. In fact, underwriters prefer you don't sell any shares at the offering. For most IPOs, existing shareholders sell less than 10 to 15 percent of the offering. That's not the instant pay day you may have expected.

However, a reasonable time after the offering you will have wonderful pieces of paper called stock certificates that your stockbroker—you'll need a stockbroker—can easily convert into cash. Converting your first stock certificates is a real high. Imagine this. You give someone a piece of paper, and in return you receive a huge pile of cash! If you're like many entrepreneurs, you'll be loving America! It's the dream come true.

The Second Sale

Assuming you are still involved with the company (most entrepreneurs who started the company for the right reasons are) and have an ownership stake, you can issue a private placement or secondary offering. In a private placement, you and the board of directors sell a portion of the company to a private investor in exchange for stock. In a secondary offering, additional stock is sold publicly through the stock exchange. In both cases, founders, employees and board members can sell significant blocks of stock during these offerings.

The Third Sale, or Selling the Company

As a founding entrepreneur, you'll probably never want to sell the company outright or for your own benefit. However, if you're a public company, the company no longer belongs to you, it belongs to the shareholders. If an offer for purchase from another company, for example, significantly enhances the value from a fiduciary standpoint, you need to seriously consider the offer with your board. You are acting in good faith in the interest of your shareholders, so it is your fiduciary responsibility, regardless of how you personally feel about selling the company.

One thing to keep in mind above all else: You are always better off if you have more than one qualified buyer. If there seems to be interest in the company, court several suitors to garner the best deal for your shareholders.

Now What?

Once the sale is over and the reality of what you've built for those around you and yourself actually sinks in, you may be left wondering what next? Ordinary life seems a little slow and subdued when contrasted with the thrill ride you've been on for the past several years. That is natural.

After the sale, take a few weeks off, maybe even a month or two. Let your body and mind quiet, and you'll discover your next step. Maybe there's an idea you've wanted to pursue and didn't have the time. If so, go do it all again. Or you may decide to help someone else through the entrepreneurial process. After all, you are now older and much, much wiser. You have a great deal to share. You can help one of your former employees, one who probably caught the entrepreneurial bug from you, get started by investing and advising.

By getting involved again, it will keep you from spending time tracking your previous company and worrying about whether or not you should have sold it. That is a meaningless activity. The sooner you proactively determine what it is you want to do and get productive doing it, the better off you and everyone around you will be. You'll begin a new phase of your existence. And the excitement will start all over again.

When you've been an investor or advisor for a few years and want to slow down, the advice is simple: Write a book, like this one, and try to help not just one person at a time, but everyone who strives to be an entrepreneur.

Bibliography

Bramson, Robert M. *Coping with Difficult People.* New York: Anchor/ Doubleday, 1981.

Collins, James C., and Jerry I. Porras. *Built to Last: Successful Habits of Visionary Companies.* New York: Harper Business, 1994.

Drucker, Peter. *Innovation and Entrepreneurship.* New York: Harper and Row, 1985.

Drucker, Peter. *Management: Tasks Responsibilities Practices.* New York: Harper and Row, 1974.

Gates, Bill. *The Road Ahead.* New York: Viking, 1995.

Laurence, J. Peter, and Raymond Hull. *The Peter Principle: Why Things Always Go Wrong.* New York: William Morrow and Company, Inc., 1969.

Lasser, J.K. *J.K. Lasser's Business Management Handbook.* New York: McGraw-Hill Book Company, 1968.

Kami, Michael J. *Trigger Points.* New York: McGraw-Hill Book Company, 1988.

Miller, Robert B., and Stephen E. Heiman. *Conceptual Selling.* Reno: Miller Heiman, Inc., 1987.

Miller, Robert B., and Stephen E. Heiman. *Strategic Selling.* Reno: Miller Heiman, Inc., 1987.

Moore, Geoffrey A. *Inside the Tornado.* New York: Harper Business, 1995.

Peters, Tom, and Nancy Austin. *A Passion for Excellence.* New York: Warner Books, 1985.

Porter, Michael E. *Competitive Advantage.* New York: The Free Press, 1985.

Rogers, William. *Think: A Biography of the Watsons and IBM.* New York: Stein and Day, 1969.

Shea, Michael. *Leadership Rules.* London: Century, 1990.

Shefsky, Lloyd E. *Entrepreneurs Are Made Not Born.* New York: McGraw-Hill Book Company, Inc., 1994.

Steiner, George A. *Strategic Planning.* New York: The Free Press, 1979.

Townsend, Robert. *Up the Organization.* New York: Alfred A. Knopf, 1970.

Uris, Auren. *Mastery of People*. New Jersey: Prentice Hall, 1964.

Webster, Bryce. *The Power of Consultative Selling*. New Jersey: Prentice Hall, 1987.

Index